S0-BJB-684

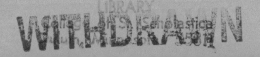

LIBRARY
College of St. Scholastica
WITHDRAWN

In Search for Community: Encounter Groups and Social Change

AAAS Selected Symposia Series

Published by Westview Press
5500 Central Avenue, Boulder, Colorado

for the

American Association for the Advancement of Science
1776 Massachusetts Ave., N.W., Washington, D.C.

In Search for Community: Encounter Groups and Social Change

⌐ Edited by Kurt W. Back ⌐

AAAS Selected Symposium   **4**

HM
134
.I5
1978

AAAS Selected Symposia Series

All rights reserved. No part of this publication may be reproduced or transmitted in any form or by any means, electronic or mechanical, including photocopy, recording, or any information storage and retrieval system, without permission in writing from the publisher.

Copyright © 1978 by the American Association for the Advancement of Science

Published in 1978 in the United States of America by

    Westview Press, Inc.
    5500 Central Avenue
    Boulder, Colorado 80301
    Frederick A. Praeger, Publisher and Editorial Director

Library of Congress Number: 77-90415
ISBN: 0-89158-431-5

Printed and bound in the United States of America

About the Book

Each society has its own ways of integrating members into its community, and in times of rapid social change these methods for asserting and continuing communities change their form and meaning. Current society has spawned new devices-- such as encounter groups and self-realization techniques-- designed to exalt community purely in terms of interpersonal relations. The contributors to this volume study this phenomenon from a cross-disciplinary point of view, drawing on the fields of anthropology, psychology, social psychology, sociology, and history. Their approach enables us to evaluate the new groups and techniques in comparison with other phenomena in the society and with rituals in other societies and times, clearly placing them in the history of ideas. The articles also provide us with a clearer understanding of the particular techniques used.

v

LIBRARY
College of St. Scholastica
Duluth, Minnesota 55811

Introductory Note

This monograph consists of papers presented at two symposia at AAAS Annual meetings, <u>Encounter Groups</u> in 1971 and <u>Encounter Groups and Social Change</u> in 1977. The three papers, "Encounter Groups: Some Empirical Issues, Explanations, and Values" by Bernard G. Rosenthal, "Sensitivity Training: Dilemmas in Paradise" by Alexander D. Blumenstiel and "'I have always depended on the kindness of strangers'" by Kurt W. Back, were given at the earlier meeting and selected for this volume because of their relevance to the current topic. They were updated and revised by the authors. The other four papers, "Passage to Community: Encounter in Evolutionary Perspective" by James W. Fernandez, "Destructive Gemeinschaft" by Richard Sennett, "Encounter Groups and Humanistic Psychology" by M. Brewster Smith, and "Communes, Encounter Groups and the Search for Community" by Benjamin D. Zablocki were given at the 1977 meeting and edited by the authors for this volume.

Contents

List of Figures

Foreword

The *AAAS Selected Symposia Series* was begun in 1977 to
provide a means for more permanently recording and more
widely disseminating some of the valuable material which is
discussed at the AAAS Annual National Meetings. The volumes
in this *Series* are based on symposia held at the Meetings
which address topics of current and continuing significance,
both within and among the sciences, and in the areas in which
science and technology impact on public policy. The *Series*
format is designed to provide for rapid dissemination of information, so the papers are not typeset but are reproduced
directly from the camera copy submitted by the authors, without copy editing. The papers are reviewed and edited by
the symposia organizers who then become the editors of the
various volumes. Most papers published in this *Series* are
original contributions which have not been previously published, although in some cases additional papers from other
sources have been added by an editor to provide a more comprehensive view of a particular topic. Symposia may be reports of new research or reviews of established work, particularly work of an interdisciplinary nature, since the AAAS
Annual Meeting typically embraces the full range of the
sciences and their societal implications.

WILLIAM D. CAREY
Executive Officer
American Association for
the Advancement of Science

About the Editor

Kurt W. Back, James B. Duke Professor of Sociology at Duke University, has conducted research in group formation and social change; the measurement of interpersonal group and elite communications; the interrelations of psychology, demography and history; and the social psychology of culture. He is the author and coauthor of many books, including Beyond Words: The Story of Sensitivity Training and the Encounter Movement *(Russell Sage, 1972).*

Introduction

Kurt W. Back

Frustrated longing for community will be readily
accepted as a predicament of contemporary society. One may
wonder why this is so. Simple explanations have been given
either that there has been an actual deprivation or that we
have a heightened awareness of human need for community.
Both seem to be off the mark. As in analogous situations
with other needs, the situation is probably more complex.
A sense of deprivation, derived from some real threat, may
lead to a frantic search of the experience itself. Like a
Don Juan, who cannot love but searches for conquests for
their own sake, we find community bereft of its wider
meaning becoming an even more compelling goal.

A currently popular point of view proclaims that the
perfect community did exist, but has been destroyed by the
development of modern technological society. This resembles
the traditional belief in a golden age or lost paradise, and
has as little foundation in actual fact. For instance,
Raymond Williams (1) has shown how the image of a perfect
integrated community has been put about one hundred years in
the past,century after century. It is likely, therefore,
that the perfect, integrated community is an ideal. In a
similar vein Burke (2) has shown that temporally prior is
frequently used as a metaphor for the logically prior, and
so the belief in the strong community in the past may well
be a metaphor for a deep-seated need for community.

The essays collected in this volume do not bemoan the
break-up of the ancient community leading to a current
frantic search to re-establish it, but they acknowledge a
peculiarity in current efforts to assuage this desire, which
really may be a new development. This new feature is the
acceptance of community for its own sake. The very facts of
membership, of interaction and of emotional response are

accepted as values in themselves. The resulting self-consciousness of group membership leads to concentration on the present situation, the minute analysis of interpersonal relations and the values of self-realization, "self" being defined mainly as body and emotions.

The clearest expressions of the search for community, as conceived in this way, are the mechanisms which have been created for group interaction and self-expression, such as encounter groups, T-groups, sensory awareness and their several variations. As specific social inventions, they belong to our time and society, although analogous groups have had a long heritage. The sessions at which these papers were presented had encounter groups as their common focus, as well as in their title. They looked at encounter groups from the perspectives of different disciplines and different empirical approaches. Each author placed this new technique into an appropriate setting, as a social, historical or personal phenomenon.

The first paper presents an anthropological perspective, showing the roots of encounter groups in a previous ritual experience. James Fernandez finds a recurrent scheme in all rituals designed to achieve community. This process has been known as rites de passage (3), and the same process can be seen as a model of the healing process (4). Typically, the function of the process is to receive a new generation or temporarily lost members into the community. First the initiates, the unintegrated members of the community, are assembled, their common fate is explained through rituals and ordeals, and they are guided to a precarious position, out of their old status and not yet into their new. This is the condition of liminality (5). The second part of the ritual is re-integration. The initiated are shown the secret traditions, ancestries and other facts and symbols which tie the individual to the society including the true members of the community. Contemporary rituals as typified by the encounter group omit the second part of this process. There is no re-integration into the larger comminity. The transition group is an aim in itself. Liminality is achieved but not transcended.

Richard Sennett shows the historical setting in which this truncated ritual has occurred. He shows the developments which have obliterated the distinction between public and private sphere since the nineteenth century and he traces the transition in two particular instances; the change from privacy to intimacy and from eroticism to sexuality. In both cases he demonstrates the triumph of the close inter-personal relation over any norms of public conduct. Self-expression becomes the ultimate aim. The twin goals of the spatially separated group and the lack of constraint on individual emotion show again the arrest at the liminal stage of the transition ritual, the formation of a community without tradition or future orientation.

Brewster Smith demonstrates an equivalent process within the science most closely concerned, namely psychology. The humanizing attempt in modern psychology was a reaction to the extreme behaviorism of the early part of the century. The founders of humanistic psychology wanted a science which would integrate the various aspects of being human, behavior as well as experiences, intellect as well as emotion, the present as well as past and future. However, within a short time this aim was deflected into the definition of humanistic psychology as the here-and-now, self-realization cult of the encounter group. Smith documents how this change occurred and how it fits into the social climate which the two previous papers described.

The next three contributions describe in greater detail the workings and present dilemmas of the intensive emotional group. Rosenthal describes, in general, the questions of techniques, outcomes and dangers of conducting the groups. He concentrates mainly on therapy groups. They are groups most directly concerned with producing individual change with a possible re-integration into society. Here the emphasis on the group membership itself becomes especially visible as a contrast to the ostensible aim.

Encounter groups are only one mechanism of the new community consciousness. A less temporary situation is the commune, the intentional community, where intimacy and sexuality become ways of life. Zablocki describes the results of his continuing study of a sample of communes. He succeeds in identifying the conditions under which members join. A large proportion of communes are designed for persons in situations for which society has made no provisions. Zablocki identifies three human situations where this lack is becoming especially acute. Under these conditions the group, though an aim in itself, can assume some permanence in a person's life.

Encounter groups reached their peak in the late 1960's. They have had to adjust themselves to changing needs of the society, and in particular, to a changing market. Blumenstiel had investigated the encounter and sensitivity training groups in their heyday, and tells what really happened during the workshops, as seen from the point of view of different participants. He is also sensitive to the lost paradise of those days and shows what has happened, how the leaders are trying to cope with the shifting scene and what the prospects are.

Literature mirrors the life of its society. The rise and decline of the encounter movement could not but leave its traces on contemporary writing. Literature puts subtle relationships into stronger relief than is otherwise possible and can give us clues to puzzling aspects of the encounter movement. Back traces the interplay of contemporary literature and the search for community. Plays and novels represent as well as influence social patterns. The history of the encounter movement seen through literature serves as a summary of the themes elaborated in this volume.

These seven papers expose the setting as well as the nature of the peculiar self-directed groups of our time. It may have been an achievement of our time to accept belonging to a group or community as an end in itself, without any further justification of an aim to be achieved through the group. However, this achievement, like technology for technology's sake, may have a hollow ring. The liminal group owes its existence as a step in the achievement of a community. Without this goal before the participants, the temporary community may not be a viable substitute for the lost chain of being, but may be an additional heavy burden to assume.

References

1. Williams, Raymond, The Country and the City. New York:
    Oxford University Press, 1973.

2. Burke, Kenneth, A Grammar of Motives. London: Routledge
    Kegan Paul, 1960.

3. Gennep, Arnold van, The Rites of Passage. London:
    Routledge Kegan Paul, 1960.

4. Frank, Jerome D., Persuasion and Healing. Baltimore:
    Johns Hopkins Press, 1961.

5. Turner, Victor W., The Ritual Process, Chicago: Aldine
    1969, and Dramas, Fields and Metaphors. Ithaca:
    Cornell University Press, 1974.

James W. Fernandez, professor of anthropology at Prince-ton University, has researched revitalization movements in Africa and the Western Mediterranean, including field work in these regions. His area of specialization is cultural anthropology.

1

Passage to Community: Encounter in Evolutionary Perspective

James W. Fernandez

> A society is similar to a house, divided into rooms and corridors. The more a society resembles our own form of civilization the thinner are its internal partitions and the more open are its doors of communications.
>
> Van Gennep, The Rites of Passage

> The neophyte in liminality must be a tabula rasa, a blank slate, on which is inscribed the knowledge and wisdom of the group, in those respects that pertain to the new states.
>
> V. Turner, The Ritual Process

Arresting and Organizing Images

A film that has frequently captured the imagination of thoughtful college students these days is Antonioni's The Passenger, though it may be that the film is more interesting to students of anthropology. The film begins, afterall, in an anthropological milieu, the desert of North Africa, in that kind of five room airstrip hotel in which many an anthropologist sweltered in the late colonial and post-colonial period. Barren as it was it was the last touch of Europe to be had before trekking out for those long months in villages beyond the third range of hills. Though the hero of this film is a reporter he has some pronouncedly anthropological type interests in "the soul of the Arab." The film even has that telling brief interview with a European educated tribesman--telling in these years of the

struggle between the objective and the subjective paradigm in
social science which is part of the struggle between culture
and counter-culture of the last decade. This struggle may
be, of course, more relevant to anthropological inquiry
where, by contrast with those among whom we inquire, our own
identities may be so much more at play. The mirror for man
we hold up may reflect us as much as the other. In any
event the tribesman replies to the reporter's question, "I
don't think you understand how little you can learn from your
questions. You can learn more about yourself than you can
learn of me from my answers." He then takes the reporter's
film camera and turns it upon its owner, "Now ask me the
same question as before" he says. That is apt for what I am
about here. With the anthropological materials in mind I am
asking questions here about community and about encounter but
with the intention of learning also about ourselves now and
in the future. For in fact these issues are difficult to
discuss independent of the position we take on the objectivity of social science inquiry or on the transformability of
American culture. Our positions on these issues affect
whether or not our imaginations are captured by the images of
encounter groups!

     This film seems to me an appropriate way to frame our
discussion for several other reasons. The hero of this
movie, a tabula rasa figure named Locke, perpetually searching the world over to write down others' words, is notably a
man without a community. He is a man so devoted to register-
ing the views of others that he cannot take responsibility
for himself or espouse his own views. He will not even take
responsibility for his own body and in effect changes his own
body for another...resigning himself as a passenger aboard
that other body until carried to his (its) fatal denouement
in a little community in southeastern Spain. Since encounter
groups characteristically ask of us that we take responsibility for ourselves and our feelings and particularly that
we accept our bodies, and since such groups characteristically ask that we be honest about the problems involved in
communing with ourselves and communicating it to others--well
it is hard to imagine a character more in need of encounter
than this disembodied globe trotting tabula rasa.

     I am also interested in this film as a framing device
for our discussion because Arnold van Genneps' classic Rites
of Passage (1) makes enduring commentary on these problems.
He did not hesitate to treat man as "a passenger" in the life
cycle, though the arena of this passage--the house metaphor
we have used as an epigraph raises this issue--is a good deal
different than the much vaster setting of our passage through
the modern world...where men and women hurrying on their

appointed rounds pursuing their over-commitments ever re-
ceding before them pass each other, endlessly transitional,
like the proverbial ships at night. It is not surprising
that encounter groups or other like groups seek as part of
their method to house, cabin up, and contain, as it were,
their participants in a limited arena of interaction for
long periods if not the duration of their interactions.
Community is in part rooming arrangements. We shall return
to this point.

I should also like to make one additional introductory
point which anthropologists, at least, cannot take for
granted--and that is the fact, I suppose that it is a very
obvious point, that our capacity for community and our need
for encounter arises from the fact that we are social animals
anxious in lonliness and driven by it. Of course it is hard
to imagine how we would have survived the pliocene let alone
come to dominate the world in the way we have if this were
not the case. (2) But the fact is not to be taken for
granted particularly by we scholars, "head trippers" in the
idiom of encounter, whose lucubrations, most frequently
occuring in self-imposed isolation in cells, cubicles, car-
rels, and studies, may cause us to overestimate our intellectual nature. Impressive indeed is the edifice of reason
in human culture. But we are still in very important measure
preoccupied like all social animals with matters having to do
with "relatedness"--domination, subordination, presence,
absence, affection, hostility, inclusion, exclusion. It is
just such matters as these that community and encounter are
all about. However we may intellectualize then they concern
the redemption of our social natures and the revitalizing of
our relatedness by the re-establishment of immediate and
vital relations with others often by ritual means. For we
are ritual animals too! It is Locke's fate perhaps not to
have recognized that fact--not to have recognized the social
impulses that permeate the blank slate of his reportorial
presence.

It is quite another question, however, as to whether
encounter groups provide an enduring and effective method for
"revitalizing our relatedness." Here I think an anthropological perspective can be brought usefully to bear. First
the anthropological literature is full of ritual institutions
very like encounter groups. For they are not, as it is sometimes said, just a phenomena of the sixties or the "unique
consequence of an utopian stream in American culture," or
"the most significant social invention of the twentieth
century." Phenomena of this kind are very probably a cultural universal. On the other hand there is something unique
about encounter groups that makes them stand out from the

anthropological materials. And we should look at this
important difference--its causes and its consequences for
their own viability and for social change.

The Encounter with Significant Others, Significant Selves

It is very widespread and it may be a universal in the
anthropological literature that the human capacity for
relatedness to others, this social animality, is not satisfied and may be more often frustrated, in the day-in and
day-out preoccupations and occupations of getting a living.
Those whose paths are crossed or with whom one cooperates in
the everyday world do not seem to fully satisfy the sense of
significant relatedness. Special occasions and special
groups are created, therefore, by means of which men and
women can come into contact with a significant other.
Indeed that encounter seems to be one of the main purposes
of ritual and ceremonial occasions.

The classic example of these special occasions is the
vision or spirit quest phenomenon particularly prominent
among North American Indians (3). For purposes of supernatural strengthening young men are released from the
requirements of social life and alone, or at most under the
tutelage of a shamen,wander out upon the landscape until in
a state of exhaustion and semi-starvation they hallucinate a
significant other--a Guardian Spirit who will watch over
them in the challenge of the adult life to come. The recent
works of Carlos Castaneda (4) imaginatively convey, better
than any strictly anthropological account, the world of
shamanistic tutelage and the wandering search, with the aid
of hallucinogens, for a significant other. Indeed the
popularity of Castaneda's work suggests that he offers, con-
current to the popularity of Encounter Groups, an alternative
vision of relatedness to men and women caught up in the
utilitarian industrial-bureaucratic world.

Much of the significant encounter in the anthropological
literature takes place in a group which, in the persons of
its priests and ritual specialists, carefully shepherds the
initiate to their encounter administering the sacra and
other symbolic stimuli which conduce to the actual image or
the felt presence of the other. This is true, for example,
of the elaborate paraphernalia that characterize the shrines
of West Africa and the sanctuaries of the Caribbean. (5) If
this symbolic paraphernalia does not actually stimulate
possession by the god or troubling spirit at the least it
provides a setting, an atmosphere, which authenticates
possession by this significant other.

These shrines and sanctuaries have, most often, a therapeutic purpose. Encounter with the significant other ministers to those who are in a state of malaise either indirectly by possessing and empowering those who are treating them or directly by their own possession. For these ritual "encounter groups" which gather at African or New World shrines vary as to whether it is the priests who are possessed or those who are consulting the shrine. Nor need dissociation take the form of possession. The rituals may lead to ecstasis in which the soul or spirit of the adept is imagined to go out from its body to meet the gods or troubling ambient spirits. In rituals influenced by ancestral cult and thus having an idea of a geneology it is as often imagined that one's essential self must be released from the body in order to meet, at least half-way, with the hovering dead (6). But in either case of dissociation, whether possession or ecstasis, the body rather than being the focus of encounter is the passive vehicle of the spiritual event which leads to its transformation. One comes to terms with one's body, ministers to it in a therapeutic way, by dissociating from it. Indeed very often these vehicles of encounter are accompanied by forms of denial of the body, abnegation, flagellation, designed to aid in the dissociation process.

These varieties of encounter with significant others take place, by and large, in societies where the kin group is the predominant reality and men and women are obliged to come to terms with that reality. They must recognize its transcendency. It is the encounter with the significant other that symbolically represents that transcendence. Men and women search out guardian spirits, troubling ancestors and errant deities all of whom have a greater reality than the searcher and whose apparition while confirming the identity of the searcher and ministering to him does so at the expense of his own significance.

All this seems to contrast sharply with Encounter Groups where the objective is, referring to various phrasings, to introduce people to their "real selves" or "to open oneself up in the face of others to all aspects of oneself." (7). So although both kinds of encounter seek meaningful relatedness that search is exocentric in most of the materials known to anthropology and endocentric in the case of Encounter Groups...which seek, as it were, the significant self rather than the significant other.

There are various reasons that account for this difference in orientation. The obvious one is that modern encounter groups take place in a western culture that puts

ontological and ideological emphasis on the reality of the
individual to a degree virtually unknown in the anthropological materials (8). Another epistemological reason is
that Encounter Groups take place in a sub-culture of that
western culture that has moved from the objective to the
subjective paradigm (9). That is it has moved from the
view that there is an empirical reality out there to be
known to an emphasis upon the constitutive and imaginative
act of the knower. The locus of knowledge has moved from
the objective world to the subjective world. Finally, and
this relates to these philosophic stances, there is a profound distrust in modern Encounter Groups of that very
society with which anthropological types of encounter groups
are seeking to come to terms and whose reality and dignity
of confidence is unquestionably accepted.

Modern encounter takes the view that much of society is
based on dishonesty (10). It is this dishonesty that is a
major reason for the existence of these groups. As Coulson
tells us in milder terms "Encounter groups began because
there didn't seem to be enough room in our highly organized
society for people to meet just as people when we weren't
playing roles...being guarded, when we weren't feeling compelled to impress one another and meet one another's expect-
tations...where performance wasn't central." (11) Such
views as these are obviously a reaction to the shift, to use
an older social science vocabulary, from a world of the
continuities and diffused and multiplex solidarities of kin
communities to the world of functionally specific contract
relations and special purpose associations. But paradoxically while modern Encounter Groups react to that shift
and the "dishonest" conditions it imposes they also espouse
the individualist, subjectivist philosophical perspectives
brought about by that shift.

We may not wish to make too much of the distinction
between encounter of the significant other as over against
encounter with the significant self. After all the significant other from a psychological perspective can be regarded as simply a projected self, an alter ego projected into a
troubling spirit, an unrequited ancestor, an insistent
deity. The other can be regarded as a ghost danced into
being as an escape from psychic crisis of one kind or
another (12). As the phenomenologists argue there is a
reflexivity in the social world between the knowing of the
self and the knowing of the other so that an absolute distinction between self and other is difficult to maintain (13)

The greater question for the anthropologist would be
whether a really enduring and transformative encounter with

enduring commitment to a significantly new self (or other) is possible without the symbols, metaphors and other "objective correlatives" by which the self and other can be truly grasped. Encounter groups endeavor to interact "just as people" free of the performance requirements of life in society. But in the anthropological material there is, almost always, some kind of ritual path or sequential scenario along which the self, inchoate in itself, is gradually led to perform its new emergent identity (14). The symbols and metaphors of this performance are crucial representations—revelatory of what it is the adept is trying to become (15). The question is whether modern encounter can be enduringly effective, as other than moments of intense emotion, without a developing, image-laden, symbol-laden scenario in which men and women believe or, at the least, in which they can suspend disbelief.

Encounter Groups often seem, however emotion laden or dramatic in one sense, literal-minded in another because of their rejection of symbolic accompaniments other than those that can be generated spontaneously by the participants. "An Encounter Group is a pretty free place where one is thrown back on one's own resources" it is argued (16). But from the anthropological perspective it might be argued that such freedom is illusory. We do not discover things by ourselves. They are revealed to us or predicated upon us out of the communities' repertoire of images. Nor do we have a significant self independent of role requirements however much the individual oriented worldview insists that we do. Encounter Group spokesmen speak of the freeing up of blocked energy (10). But in the anthropological materials that energy is most effectively freed up by investment in symbolic and metaphoric vehicles of knowledge which when, interacted with, both release wisdom and act as plans for subsequent behavior.

It is now an accepted fact that the so-called "high learners" in Encounter Groups are a minority—often a very reduced one (17). For most participants the experience seems to be transitory or negative. An anthropological explanation would be that there can be no enduring and predictable encounter without an established dramaturgy that serves not only as a repository of knowledge but also has an important "distancing" function. For the emotions of others and of the self experienced too directly, as is often the case in Encounter Groups, are too disturbing and tension-producing, to produce an enduring encounter of transcendent significance.

In short anthropological arguments would hold that

significance in self and in others is the consequence of
dramatic scenarios in which persons can interact with powerful collective representations which are the source of that
significance. Encounter groups would be then, effective to
the degree that the self-revelations they encourage produce
truly effective representations for collective contemplation.
And they are enduringly effective to the degree that they
institutionalize such representations.

Intensification

Van Gennep was primarily interested in those disturb-
ances--the individual life crises--produced by passage from
one status, one chamber to use his metaphor, to another.
The rites of passage which he discussed acted to incorporate
individuals into new statuses by forcably separating them
from the old, passing them through the bizarre and dissociating experiences of a transitional or liminal condition
and then reintegrating them with a changed identity apt to
their new challenges back into the community. It can also
be argued, as we have above, that rites of passage create
significantly new selves by bringing former selves dramatically into contact with significant others.

The focus on the individual's life crisis, however,
needed to be complimented with the notion of group crisis
and the periodic need that all groups experience for re-
invigorating their relatedness not as a consequence of moving
through the chambers of life but simply as a consequence of
having social relatedness fall out of kilter with the passage
of time and the passage of seasons. Chappel and Coon (18)
introduced the notion of "rites of intensification." These
were rituals designed to deal with disturbances in what they
called "interaction rates" with the object of returning
members of a group to appropriate interaction. However
difficult may be to find the baseline for measuring appropriate interaction rates the notion of intensification in
the relatedness of persons is an important aspect of the
anthropological view of encounter.

Here are some examples of intensification of relationships which occur in the community creating movements with
which I have been working. In the Bwiti religion of western
equatorial Africa the entire membership at mid-night, after
an evening of dancing out their various roles, form a line
and each holding a candle file out into the forest seeking
any remaining ancestors. Returning then to the village the
line of members commences to wind a circle tighter and
tighter until all the members are compressed solidly

together and the candles held above their heads make virtually one flame. They intone "we are one heart." After this
the members break rapidly apart, virtually centrifugally
into their respective ritual spheres. (19)

In contrast to this compaction of the members--an
intensification by compression--take another circle in use
among Zulu Zionists of southern Africa. (20) These are
smaller groups of men and women who worship over several
hours time in grass circles in the vacant lots of South
African cities. They worship in most important part by
running around the outer circle at an increasingly verti-
ginous pace. Those who are impure or need purification will
be thrown centrifugally out of the circle. Those most pure
and blessed may be drawn into the vacuous center where the
Holy Spirit dwells for a confirming encounter with it. But
for most members effective worship consists in a lengthy
circling about at a highly coordinated and intense pace.

Intensification of relationship need not be corporeal or
by highly coordinated kinesthetic activity. In the Chrisian-
isme Celeste religion of southern Dahomey, now Benin, the
reading of bible passages in highly coordinated chorus--in
impressive if relatively mindless unison--accomplishes an
intensification of relationship by group discharge of an
"intellectual" task. The style of intensification of interaction is quite different in these three cases--centripetal,
centrifugal, mental--but in every case there is a high
degree of coordination which if not expressive of optimum
interaction is at least suggestive of it.

In the anthropological literature the experience of the
affective recreation and maintenance of community depends,
in part, upon periodic intensification of this kind.
Encounter Groups insofar as they achieve this kind of
coordination of group energy would be, by anthropological
standards, affective agents of community. But insofar as a
primary value among them is careful preservation of the
spontaneous expressions of selves and careful cultivation of
the blocked energy of individuals without the strict requirement of coordination of group energy, then their product will
more likely be the therapy of individuals rather than the
creation of community. For if community is not actually
created by highly coordinated interaction it is at least
suggested and symbolized, by insignia, sign or signal, as an
emergent whole. In highly coordinated interaction the
individual encounters himself as a part caught up and rapidly
fusing into the highly significant whole.

Returning to the Whole

Encounter Groups lay emphasis, and in this they are
influenced by Gestalt Therapy (21), upon the participants'
achieving a wholeness if not by getting in touch with those
parts of the self suppressed or repressed in the modern
production-line society at least by accepting his or her
missing parts as non-essential to wholeness. There is also
an effort to obtain awareness of the whole group as a positive dynamic entity though this emphasis upon group dynamics
has been variable and a declining emphasis in recent years
in the T-Group-Encounter Group Movement--perhaps for reasons
discussed in the previous section.

But the partness of experience or the obligation in the
work-a-day world of engaging only a part of the self is not
a uniquely modern condition. Though it is undoubtedly
exacerbated by an evolving differentiation of structure and
specialization of function in society. In most of the
arenas of encounter in the anthropological literature we see
attempts to bring the participants into a higher order of
integration of experience than the everyday. This is done
both in respect to the experience of themselves and in
respect to the relation between themselves and the social
and cosmic levels of experience. In fact, it must be
argued from the anthropological perspective that there is
no real encounter with wholeness that does not, at least,
knit together the psycho-physiological self and the social
order. This point has been made frequently in the literature. (22) It is pointed out that efficacious religious
activity unites personal sentiments, moods and motivations,
to the structure of social obligations. Indeed the definition of a religious symbol in Victor Turner's view is a
representation that has at once a physiologic (orectic) and
a social (normative) referent. (23)

This task of integration or "returning to the whole"
begins with the "stripping down" and "knitting together" of
the body itself. Ritual nakedness in rites of passage is
frequent. Since clothing of any kind acts to highlight
certain parts of the body while concealing other parts and
since clothing also carries the constrictions of status, it
is only by stripping that the whole body can be engaged as
"prima materia" for encounter. But the rituals do not stop
with the stripping and touching of that prima materia, however important that touching may be for Encounter Groups in
their reactions to the mechanical and abbreviated nurtur-
ance of modern life. Most often having laid out or laid
open the body, the rituals move quickly to the "knitting
together" stage. Initiates may actually count up the parts

of their body thus integrating it in anklebone-shinbone-
thighbone-backbone fashion in preparation for the new status which is to be assumed. (24)

Rituals having to do with the integration or reintegration of body parts are widespread. This "knitting together"
of the stripped, laid-out, or figuratively dismembered body
is frequently projected into the macrocosm. This is the
case of such culture heroes as the Egyptian Osiris or the
Indian Parrati. For their sacrified bodies are scattered
out and become identified with, and make fertile, various
parts of the nation. It is the yearly ritual cycle which
operates to reintegrate their bodies. It is at the same
time a reintegration of the nation. A similar kind of
knitting together occurs in Indo-European astrology. The
sun makes its annual passage through the heavenly houses.
Each of these is associated with a body part as also with
parts of the great heavenly body. Thus in the course of a
year's time both the individual and the world body is made
whole by cyclical consultation of body parts at both the
microcosmic and the macrocosmic levels.

This knitting together of the microcosm and the
macrocosm is most pronounced in Hindi ritual practice
where the notion of the cosmos as divine body serves to
orient individual ritual practice. If one is careful in
one's own body alignments and if one follows appropriate
ritual sequences, an actual merging of body and cosmos can
occur. This knitting together of one's own body parts with
the cosmos is seen in a series of "mantras"--powerful verses--
recited by temple priests or initiates seeking release from
particularity to the larger wholeness. By a series of hand
gestures during ritual recitations at once to parts of the
heavens as to parts of the body, the incomplete image of
cosmic divinity becomes complete and vital. But at the
same time the priest or worshipper's own body is brought
to ritual completion--returned to the whole in the fullest
sense. (25)

There are many other examples of microcosm-macrocosm
associations in the anthropological literature. Lévi-
Strauss has shown how a shaman sorcerer, in the process of
ministering to a woman with a difficult pregancy, imaginatively expands her womb until it becomes identified with
the orderly cosmos--whose order is then returned to the
womb. (26) And Lamphere has shown a similar process with
the Navaho who concentrate, in the therapeutic process, on
ordering the cosmos and then transfering that order back to
the afflicted body. (27) But we are not obliged to seek
these microcosm-macrocosm examples only in the cross-

cultural literature. La·ing has shown how the members of a
family can take up residence in the various parts of a disturbed woman's body, the father in the tongue, the brother in
the chest, the baby in the hand, and that therapy for psychic
stress consists in the acting out of harmonious relations
between these personified parts. (28)   And Douglas has argued
that we grasp our corporeality in terms of society. In our
body is the image of our society and we are constrained to
present our bodies and administer their processes according
to the kind of administrative structure valued by society.
(29)

These are all metaphoric processes in which one domain
or level of experience comes, by similarity, to stand for or
be intended in another. Day in and day out in life we live
sequentially, metonymically, in cause and effect fashion
with, at most, the part standing for the whole without being
it. But as Lévi-Strauss has argued in the imaginative life
of the mind, in fantasy but particularly in myth and ritual,
we move back and forth between metonymic commitments to the
sequential exploration and fulfillment of the contiguous
parts of a given domain of experience and the assertion by
similarity, that is, by metaphoric association, of entirely
other domains of interest. While metonymy is the mode of
thought which explores parts, metaphor "returns to the
whole." The accumulation of these metaphoric assertions
into metonymic activity enables us to discover in the
fullest sense the universe in the body and the body in the
universe. (30)

Rituals of passage and intensification in the anthropological literature are fruitfully analyzed, then, as the
acting out of metonymic and metaphoric modes of thought...
as a process of encountering and exploring parts of selves
and then finding these parts associated to, projected, and
transformed into greater wholes. This movement back and
forth between parts and wholes and between levels is the
essential movement of the ritual process and it is where the
sensation of wholeness lies.

While the body is the primordial vehicle of these imaginative excursions, it is not in and of itself sufficient to
its own wholeness and, from the anthropological view, it is
illusory to expect that the body can become whole at its own
level and at its core simply by stripping away all the
accretions of its social nature, its unhealthy patterns of
acting in a dishonest society. (31) Images from other
orders of existence must be associated to it, predicated
upon it, which suggest its resonance in these other realms
and which can act as plans for its performances. It is

simply that the body lives in society and the world and must find itself, encounter itself, in these other realms. Insofar as Encounter Groups mistrust society and ignore its presence in body or eschew symbolic statements by which macrocosm is shown in microcosm and parts related to wholes, to that degree the "return to the whole" will be insufficient. It may be simulated in the intense emotional fulfillment of the moment perhaps but it will remain, essentially, confined to the arena in which it occurs and not relevant to other realms of experience in which the body resonates and which, in the end, are a part of its wholeness by which it escapes its alienation.

Scenarios of Passage

The metonymic and metaphoric play of mind through images and symbols that occurs in the ritual situations of significant encounter in the anthropological literature is crucial. It affects and energizes the transition and transformation which is accomplished in these rites. For it is these images and symbols which adumbrate and figure forth the significant other, whether ancestor, deity, group or cosmos, and relate it to the participant. In the condensation of meanings characteristic of these images and symbols there is intensification, while in the multivocality of that condensation there is the possibility of bodying forth in the same configuration parts and wholes, microcosms and macrocosms.

But it would be a libel on group processes of the Encounter Group type to suppose that however body-oriented and determinedly non-verbal they may be, they do not generate symbols and metaphors which associate what is happening in the group process with other levels and domains of experience. They do! And though these spontaneously generated images may not achieve enduring status as collective representations, yet as Slater has argued, with the benefit of actual material taken from sensitivity training groups, the images and metaphors generated in these groups "draw upon a rich cultural heritage in expressing and maintaining a complex set of personal interrelationships." (32) These expressions turn out to be very like figurative solutions long adopted by men and women in groups. "A training group recapitulates cultural evolution," Slater argues. Group ontogeny recapitulates mythological phylogeny. This is another way of arguing for the relevance of the anthropological data. It is not data of the kind introduced here, however, for Slater's scenario of cultural evolution by which he organizes the group images is analytic and makes use of either the Freudian scenario of the Primal Horde sacrifice or of Erich Neumann's Great Mother scenario of Group Differentiation and Individuation.

Slater argues that the main tension and producer of the dynamic of groups is the question of boundaries--of boundary establishment and boundary maintenance--since in any process of group formation the individual has the problem of what part of himself he is going to commit to the group. After all, he has other parts of himself committed elsewhere. How is he going to maintain the boundary between that commitment and others? For the group the boundary question concerns the relation of its activities to the larger society of which it is a part. Bringing the anthropological materials to bear here is fruitful. For Encounter Groups in modern society in contrast to ritual groups in communal society seek a total and uninhibited commitment of the individual--the dissolution of all boundaries maintained in him or her which would restrain participation. At the same time, such Groups can largely avoid by isolation the problem of boundary relations with the larger society first because that larger society is considered oppressive, dishonest, constricting, or illegitimate in respect to personal core value and second because group members are usually drawn from such diverse walks of life, though generally middle class, and such dispersed geographic areas of belonging that there is no larger community to which they all belong and which binds them except in the most abstract sense. That is, the presence and gravitational attraction of the larger community is not a problem as it is in rites of passage.

Indeed, in contrast to rituals of passage or intensification, modern Encounter Groups attempt to create their own self sufficient communities for the duration of encounter. This can be seen when we contrast the scenario of Encounter Group development envisioned by Shutz, Inclusion, Control, Affection and Separation (33) with the classic Van Gennep formulation of the anthropological materials: Separation, Transition and Reintegration or Reincorporation.

The Encounter Group scenario is virtually the reverse process emphasizing inclusion first rather than separation. Separation comes last rather than reincorporation or inclusion. The emphasis on Separation first in rituals of passage is a testimoney to the reality of the larger community from which separation must be effected and whose superordinate presence throughout the rituals is an important part of the experience of the initiates. This larger community, in whose presence and for whose more effective solidarity the rites are being performed, exerts its lines of force producing boundary tension and making the initiates' isolation an even more significant achievement.

For modern Encounter Groups there is no meaningful
larger community to which participants all belong, hence
no great problem of separation. In a very real sense the
Encounter Group is community for the participants who are
otherwise involved as passengers in the endless relatively
unmarked transitions of modern life while rites of passage
are moments of transition, of passenger status, for those
who are structurally committed and settled participants in
an existent community.

In Encounter Groups the emphasis is on inclusion into
what should become for the duration of the encounter a
totally preoccupying reality--so preoccupying that it
creates final problems of separation. The focus of these
modern groups is thus very much endocentric to the degree
that the problem arises of their being too sui generis, too
encapsulated, and too much of a pseudo-event vis-à-vis their
relevance to the larger society, whether community or not, of
which they are a part. It is just this relevance that we
seek to assess here in this colloquium.

For the ritual forms of encounter, in the anthropological literature, the question of relevance to the larger
society hardly arises. The community is there constantly
throughout the rites creating tension in the initiates and
in the boundaries created. It is the whole from which they
have all come, the whole which they explore and return to
symbolically in the ritual, and it is the whole into which
they will sooner or later be reincorporated.

Discussion: "Autos de Fe"--"Autos de Me"

We have consulted some of the anthropological materials
on ritual with the idea of encounter in mind: encounter with
the significant other, with the re-intensified group, with
the inter-reflectivity of microcosm-macrocosm, and with the
absence and sudden presence of community. Though some caution is in order about these generalizations, after all
the anthropological literature is vast and diverse (there
is also much diversity in the Human Potential-Encounter
Group Movement),   it seems clear enough that the rituals
of relatedness which we have reviewed are all transitions
in the life of a pre-existent and post-existent community.
Their main purpose is to provide a framework rich in the
symbolic repositories of group wisdom, such as icons,
images, metaphors, which will conduce to new forms of
relatedness or optimally return to old forms. It is these
vehicles of meaning primarily which carry that wisdom and

which, when impressed upon the "tabula rasa" of the initiates, conduce to restoration or transformation of their
relatedness.

Encounter Groups are also ritual experiences. But they
take place where there is no pre-existent or post-existent
community. They are community for their duration. Nor do
they treat the initiate as a "tabula rasa"...but rather as
an important source of wisdom about himself and about others
which must in all frankness be opened up and become a part
of the culture of this temporary community. This cultivation of individual potential makes the encounter group
rituals a great deal less predictable than the rituals of
relatedness known to anthropologists whose characteristic
is stereotyping and rigidity. And of course from the anthropological perspective Encounter Groups seem very self-
indulgent and loquacious even though they may emphasize the
non-verbal and the frank exposure of self-indulgent views.

Encounter Groups might be seen by an anthropologist as
a life crisis ritual specific to the western and more particularly American civilization of the mid-twentieth century--
before the energy crisis--which have evolved to such differentiation of structure and specialization of function and
such mobility, affluence, and secularization of outlook and
life style (34) as to have lost both the onerousness of community, on the one hand, and the satisfactions of community,
on the other. The particularity of Encounter Groups strikes
most forcibly when an anthropologist tries to imagine the
peasant or subsistent communities in the literature entering
into Encounter however given they may be to "rituals of
relatedness." One cannot imagine it!

It is easy to see why. The inhabitants of the little
communities which anthropologists have studied live, in many
respects, in an enormous room. If the more apt metaphor is
that of the house, as in the epigraph from Van Gennep, it is
still a house with very thin partitions. The awareness of
others is constantly present simply at the physical level
not to mention the psychic level where one is constantly
reminded of longstanding family rivalries and resentments.
In such a situation men and women learn to erect psychological barriers, various forms of institutionalized ignorance
and avoidance, in order not to be overwhelmed by the sheer
presence of relationships steeped with the ambivalences
accumulated over generations. They have had to learn formal-
ities and circumspections in order to prevent that enormous
room from becoming uninhabitable.

In our society despite the mobility and the transience

of our public lives--their passenger quality--in our private
lives we live most often in hermetic isolation within sound-
proof people-proof walls. In such conditions of insulation
we can, as members of little communities cannot in their
constant availability to each other, afford, indeed desire
to escape our encapsulation through encounter. No doubt
there is a principle here involving optimum interaction
rates, domestic envelopes and an inverse relationship
between physical isolation and the possibility of psychic
exteriorization.

It is not hard to appreciate why the members of communities known to anthropologists would find Encounter Groups
a near impossibility. They have already for generations
been sharing, sometimes against their will and sometimes
with the wicked relish of gossip, intimate details of their
neighbors' lives. In a sense Encounter Groups in their
frank exploration of the emotional details of lives would
be a redundant if not repugnant exercise. Community members
are already too "open-minded" to the details of their
neighbors' lives to embark upon encounter. But in another
sense they are too closed-minded and defensive. The
enmities of generations which have largely risen around
competition for limited goods (35) have been too clearly
identified and too attached to persons to make it easy to
accept attempts at open and frank declaration from one who
may have long been identified as an agent of family mis-
fortune. Encounter Groups work best among those who have
not developed a history of established enmities and inad-
vertent intimacies...who have not lived too closely together
nor had to struggle too long with "limited good."

There is another important reason why personalistic
encounter is difficult to conceive in the little communities
known to anthropology. Such communities are characteristically inimical to individual assertion and have developed
many mechanisms to prevent it. A man of one part let alone
many parts has a very difficult time developing that part
in such communities without being accused of unacceptable
egotism. Mockery, gossip, or other mechanisms are calculated to return and re-direct such an individual very
quickly to the whole community and the significant other--
away from the significant self.

This is nothing more than to say perhaps that Encounter
Groups, however they may emphasize group experience, are still
conducted very much in the idiom of the western culture of
generalized and capitalized individualism. In this culture
the emphasis is upon being responsible for oneself--on
growing oneself up rather than being grown up. Whereas it

was precisely the intent of the more traditional rites to
absolve that responsibility by intensified encounter with
the other. And while one's existential individual condition might be transitorily revealed by stripping in these
older rites it was at once absorbed, confronted, mitigated,
and ascribed to a higher reality. For if participants were
stripped to the "tabula rasa" condition they were very
quickly then written upon dramatically by the icons, symbols,
and sacra of their cultures which was unambiguously manag-
ing them, leading them through the rites in the interests
of restoring community if not cosmos. They were, in short,
"autos de fe" and not, as are Encounter Groups, "autos de
me."

It may be more correct to say that rather than seeking
to create community where none exists--although communities
have sprung up around the Encounter enterprise such as the
Esalen Institutes--that Encounter Groups are seeking to
institutionalize what Victor Turner has called, elaborating
on Van Gennep, "comunitas." (36) Turner speaks of that
unending dialectic between "societas" and "comunitas,"
between that condition, which social life requires, of the
person confined in a structure of roles and separated from
others by hierarchy and classification and property and
that condition where the person is freed up to reside in his
existential organism condition--his elemental humanity
within the generic human bond. In society the individual is
only very uncertainly perceived behind his statuses and
roles--and that is even more the case of highly organized
societies however they may proclaim individualism as the
keystone of their character. In "comunitas," however
idiosyncratic individuals may be in physical and mental
endowment, they can all come to share a common humanity.
Though Turner may over-emphasize the presence of "comunitas"
in the anthropological materials it is certainly there. And
the features he suggests for it are even more clearly present
in Encounter Groups: leveling, humbling, stripping, apparent
spontaneity, sensuality, sanctioning of otherwise unpardon-
able behavior, organismic focus, hallucination, anonymity,
violation of social rules, body engagement. All these
things are very ancient features of the dialectic of the
human condition and a manifestation of what Van Gennep
called "the law of life and of the universe" where the
energy found in any system gradually becomes spent or
locked up and must be periodically renewed and released. (37)

To have touched base with our common humanity is no
mean achievement. The effort to do so in Encounter Groups
and in such a pronounced way shows an ancient energy restoring wisdom raised to an ambitious power. One should not,

however, be fooled into believing that community can be
easily created out of "comunitas" where none exists or that
the particular characteristic of "comunitas" can be easily
generalized into society. Since time immemorial men have
harbored the vision of converting "comunitas"--profound
sympathetic relatedness--into an enduring condition--of
converting "comunitas" into community on a permanent basis.
This is the millenarian hope--the apocalyptic vision. Is
it any more probable today than it ever was?

In certain ways it may be. The very mobility and
transient, passenger quality of life in modern societies
would seem to be as propitious as any social situation could
be for frequent realizations of our existential and primordial humanity. If one can accept that there is such a
thing in modern life as "community without propinquity"
(38) such a community would have the best chance of bearing
higher levels of inter-personal sensitivity. For it is the
rule of propinquity coupled with the struggle for "limited
good" that has burdened traditional communities with the
family enmities of many generations and the surfeit of
inescapable intimacies making it necessary to confine
"comunitas" to rites of passage. There is some evidence
(39) that some members of Encounter Groups, the "high
changers" or "high learners," do carry their new sensitivity
and capacity for relatedness into their lives in associations
beyond the Group. And given the highly utilitarian and
instrumental orientation of modern life, it can surely benefit from such humanization.

But what of post-industrial communities, communities
that once again, as we are already beginning to see, will
be living with much more limited good, with less affluence
and less mobility--living, that is, without the very conditions that make "communities without propinquity" possible.
Very simply the degree to which post-industrial societies
are less affluent and mobile and thus approach, reverting to
type, the settled pre-industrial communities of limited good,
to that degree one can predict that they will be less hos-
pitable to experience of Encounter Group type.

But such a prediction makes several assumptions: 1.
That in ultimate matters having to do with "wholeness" and
"encounter" and "communing with community," the human
requirement for analogic communication in collective representations is constant; 2. that human nature will continue
to have a more or less constant capacity for intense non-
familial intimacy--more where there is affluence and mobility, less where there is limited good and propinquity; 3.
that the level of social and cultural integration from which

we regard these phenomena and the ethos and worldview characteristic of it is an enduring reality. Any suddenly
flourishing institution in human affairs always holds out
the promise of a fundamental transformation of human nature.
But one should look more fixedly at what the probabilities
are.

Conclusion: Of Evolutionary Potentials and Transformations of Worldview

I will hold to the first assumption, despite the widespread belief that the evolution of culture (and the revo-
lutions of writing and scientific method) has conclusively
brought rationality into human affairs along with increased
analysis and increased abstraction. In respect to encounter
with the profoundest human experiences, the experiences of
relatedness, any enduring communication to self or other
must be symbolic and collective. There must be skepticism
that any movement which seeks to penetrate to the level of
unstructured existential humanity and which relies primar-
ily--and then only fleetingly because of the restless search
for novelty--on the signs, symbols, and personal sacra generated spontaneously by individual members under the non-
directive guidance of individualistic leaders can effectively convey that experience with import for social change.
For such conveyance, it is to be argued, rests upon a set
of collective representations dramatically enacted in a
highly coordinated manner by the membership. Such representations are the repository of the wisdom of the group
about ultimate things. They constitute the primary evidence for what it has achieved as they are the models for
its continuing achievement--its continuing affective activity. A movement which has achieved new feelings and attitudes to be taken towards the self and towards others, new
modes of being and behaving, and which wishes to affect the
larger society with these feelings, attitudes, and modes
must arrest that larger society with convincing images
around which behaviour can be organized.

There is no doubt that Encounter Groups can be therapeutic for individuals. But is it every individual or
rather those who are especially self-exploring and exterior-
izing and with enough resilience for highly emotional self-
examination and cross-examination? It is uncertain that
that resilience is widespread in any population or can
easily be made more so even under conditions of affluence
and mobility. For most men and women in most social circumstances, Encounter Groups would seem to be an uncertainly
predictable and uncertainly communicable experience and for
that reason a declining enthusiasm rather than an enduring

transforming commitment. In that respect while Encounter Groups are surely signs of the times, as they are surely assuagements to the times, one can wonder whether they are really shapers of the times, that is, sign-givers to the times.

The question of "shaping the times" involves assumptions about the endurance of institutions and the endurance of human emotional capacities. There is, for example, enduring debate in the West (in the East the view is quite unambiguous) as to whether significant transformation of worldview can be brought about without the drastic overturning of institutions. Taking the view that it cannot be forecloses one's view of the human potential phenomenon. For they seek change by expanding and generalizing human sensitivity--by affectionate persuasion, as it were, to use a term from a key phrase in their scenario of relatedness.

With this objective in mind it is relevant to compare Encounter Groups to the Quakers. Both are perfectionist movements seeking to perfect the human potential for friendly and affectionate relatedness. Both are "experimentalist" which reject conformity to external symbolic forms and seek the spontaneous guidance of internal lights and feelings. (This, it follows from the argument made here, is one reason, other than the perfectionism, why the Quakers have always remained a small communion.)

Of course the emotive element in Encounter, the organismic focus, the range of experimentation, and the propagandistic recruitment, is all very different from the Quakers. Nevertheless there is a similarity in the belief that more perfect examples can diffuse into society-changing worldviews without a direct assault on institutions. The Quakers have created their own institutions of notable effectiveness in ameliorating the human condition, the American Friends Service Committee, for example...something which Encounter Groups have not achieved and barely attempted.

The question arises as to the evolutionary potential of these movements. For the Quakers, Boulding argues, are a social mutation out of step with times present but containing the seed of the comity and community which will characterize the post-industrial society.(40) One of the reasons that the Quakers have endured and maintained their evolutionary potential, he suggests, is because they have quietly institutionalized their business affairs and their mission. They have avoided the exhaustion of potential by emotional excess as characterizes so many perfectionist movements. Though Boulding does not have Encounter Groups in mind the

point is relevant. Do they exhaust their evolutionary potential and their mission in the high emotionality of the
encounter itself?

Even granting the Quakers greater evolutionary potential, the question still arises as to their effect upon the
powerfully striving and driven (control-oriented) worldview
of Western society. The question is even more pertinent to
Encounter Groups which in their emphasis on self-awareness
and individual experience seem to re-affirm if not celebrate
the central element in that worldview, individualism. (41)

Answers to these questions are usually thought to
respond to one's native optimism or pessimism, or what
amounts to the same thing, conservatism or progressivism.
But what is really involved is one's view of the permanence
of the human capacity for non-family intimacy such as we now
know that capacity, and the permanence of the Western social
and economic order such as we now know it. About the capacity for intimacy we may well need more "tests." If we
have "tested" Encounter Groups in this paper in traditional
communities and in modern "communities without propinquity"
there is at least one other possibility: the new communities
of contemporary China. And indeed in the Hsiao-tsu groups in
Chinese communes (42) one sees something very similar to
human potential groups. What levels of sustained intimacy
and responsive affectionate feedback do they achieve?

References and Notes

1. A. Van Gennep, The Rites of Passage (Univ. of Chicago Press, Chicago, 1960).
2. D. A. Hamburg, "Emotions in the Perspective of Human Evolution" in Expression of the Emotions, P. H. Knapp, Ed. (Int. Univ. Press, New York, 1963), pp. 246-257.
3. R. Benedict, The Concept of the Guardian Spirit in North America (American Anthropological Association Memoir, New York, 1923).
4. C. Castaneda, The Teachings of Don Juan: A Yaqui Way of Knowledge (Ballentine Books, 1968). A Separate Reality: Further Conversations with Don Juan (Pocket Books, New York, 1972).
5. M. Field, Search for Security: An Ethno-Psychiatric Study of Rural Ghana (Faber, London, 1960). A. Métraux, Voodoo in Haiti (Oxford Press, New York, 1959).
6. J. Fernandez, "T. eboga: Narcotic Ecstasis and the Work of the Ancestors" in The Flesh of the Gods, P. Furst, Ed. (Praeger, New York, 1972), pp. 237-260.
7. W.R. Coulson, Groups, Gimmicks and Instant Gurus (Harper & Row, New York and Evanston, 1972), p. 4.
8. L. Dumont, "The Modern Conception of the Individual: Notes on Its Genesis and That of Concomitant Institutions," in Contributions to Indian Sociology #8, October 1965, pp. 220-260. M. Sahlins, The Use and Abuse of Biology (Univ. of Michigan Press, Ann Arbor, 1976), pp. 93-107.
9. D. Bleich, "The Subjective Paradigm in Science Psychology and Criticism," New Literary History, Winter 1976, pp. 313-334.
10. W. C. Schutz, Elements of Encounter (Bantam Books, New York, 1973), passim.
11. W. R. Coulson, op. cit., p. 5.
12. W. LaBarre, The Ghost Dance (Doubleday, Garden City, 1970).
13. A. Schutz, The Phenomenology of the Social World (Northwestern Univ. Press, Evanston, 1967).
14. J. Fernandez, "The Mission of Metaphor in Expressive Culture," Current Anthropology, Vol. 15, #2, June 1974, pp. 119-145.
15. F. Barth, Ritual and Knowledge Among the Baktaman of New Guinea (Yale Univ. Press, New Haven, 1975).
16. W. R. Coulson, op. cit., p. 5.
17. It has always, admittedly, been difficult to measure the impact of the Encounter Experience for it depends on whose perspective, leaders' or participants', and time of measurement, right after or six months later. Lieberman et al. find only modest gain on a variety of measures and then only for a third of the participants.

M. A. Lieberman, I. D. Yalum, M. B. Miles, Encounter Groups: First Facts (Basic Books, New York, 1973), Ch. 3.

18. E. Chapple and C. Coon, Principles of Anthropology (H. Holt, New York, 1942).

19. J. Fernandez, "The Remembrance of Things Past: Alar Ayong and Bwiti as Movements of Protest in Western Equatorial Africa" in Protest and Power in Black Africa, A. Mazni, R. Rotberg, Eds. (Oxford Univ. Press, New York, 1970), pp. 427-457.

20. J. Fernandez, "Zulu Zionism," Natural History, June-July 1971, pp. 44-51.

21. F. Perl, Gestalt Therapy Verbatim (Real People Press, Lafayette, Calif., 1969).

22. P. Berger, The Sacred Canopy: Elements of a Sociological Theory of Religion (Doubleday, New York, 1967). C. Geertz, "Religion as a Cultural System" in Anthropological Approaches to the Study of Religion, ASA Monographs #3 (Tavistock, London, 1965), pp. 167-178.

23. V. Turner, The Forest of Symbols: Aspects of Ndembu Ritual (Cornell Univ. Press, Ithaca, 1967), pp. 20-21.

24. G. Tessman, Die Pangwe, Vol. II (Munster Verlag, Berlin, 1913), p. 57.

25. B. E. F. Beck, "The Symbolic Merger of Body, Space and Cosmos in Hindu Tamiland" (ms. 1975), p. 25.

26. C. Lévi-Strauss, "The Effectiveness of Symbols" in Structural Anthropology (Doubleday Anchor, New York, 1967), pp. 180-201.

27. L. Lamphere, "Symbolic Elements in Navajo Ritual," Southwest Journal of Anthropology, Vol. 25, #3, 1969, pp. 279-303.

28. R. Laing, Self and Other (Penguin Books, New York, 1969), pp. 68-71.

29. M. Douglas, Natural Symbols (Vintage Books, New York, 1970), pp. 11-18.

30. C. Lévi-Strauss, The Savage Mind (Univ. of Chicago Press, Chicago, 1965), p. 263.

31. F. Perl, op. cit., passim.

32. P. Slater, Microcosm: Structural Psychological and Religious Evolution in Groups (John Wiley, New York, 1966), pp. 234-235.

33. W. Schutz, op. cit., pp. 44-53.

34. These are the three main conditions of modern life advanced by Kurt Back to explain the success of human potential type movements. Beyond Words (Russell Sage, New York, 1972), pp. 31-40.

35. G. Foster, "Peasant Society and the Image of Limited Good," American Anthropologist, Vol. 67, #2, April 1965, pp. 300-323.

36. V. Turner, The Ritual Process (Aldine, Chicago, 1969), Chs. 3 and 4.

37. A. Van Gennep, op. cit., ix.
38. M. Webber, "Communities Without Propinquity" in Environmental Psychology: Man and His Physical Setting, H.M. Przoshansky, W. Ittelson, and L. G. Rivlin, Eds. (Holt, Rinehart, New York, 1970), pp. 334-360.
39. R. Holloman, "Ritual Opening and Individual Transformation: Rites of Passage at Esalen," American Anthropologist, Vol. 76, #2, June 1974, pp. 265-280.
40. K. Boulding, The Evolutionary Potential of Quakerism (Pendle Hill Press, Philadelphia, 1964).
41. Holloman (op. cit., pp. 276-277) argues that Encounter Groups do effect a change in worldview: mind/body dualism to unity of body and mind, emphasis on emotional control to emphasis on self-awareness and expression of emotion, competition to "comunitas," etc. But in her conclusion she recognizes the justice of the view that in their focus on the individual they reinforce a central tendency in American life. She makes reference to the observations on this point by F. L. K. Hsu--an appropriate reference insofar as Holloman argues that Encounter Groups are moving, principally, from a Western to an Eastern worldview. F. L. K. Hsu, Americans and Chinese (Natural History Press, New York, 1970).
42. M. K. Whyte, Small Groups and Political Rituals in China (U. Cal. Press, Berkeley, 1974), p. 15.
43. Some of the research reported here was supported by grants from the Ford Foundation and the Social Science Research Council. I thank Barbara Frankel and John Weatherley for helpful commentary.

Richard Sennett, director of the Center for Humanistic Studies and professor of sociology at New York University, specializes in social psychology. He is the author of **The Fall of Public Man** *(Knopf, 1977).*

2

Destructive Gemeinschaft

Richard Sennett

Every generation engages in a life-long struggle with
what it first believed. Sometimes people repudiate early
ideals, but their temperament remains unchanged, as, for
example, those rigid Stalinists who have become fiercely
anti-Marxist. In other generations, like our own, the
first truths are not challenged explicitly, rather they are
affirmed with a voice that grows ever more tired, weak, and
resigned.

The truth to which our generation assents is that psychological self-exposure is a moral good. In this view it
is better to show your feelings to another person, no matter
how wounding the feelings are, than to suppress or disguise
what you feel. A person is not being authentic with you
unless he or she is willing to share his or her secrets.
This compulsion to expose the self shows up in many different ways: it is the rationale of the feeling-industry,
from Esalen to rolfing to encounter weekends at hotels in
the Catskills. It is the rationale of the modern biography
or autobiography, in which exposure of the subject's intimate affairs is presumed to have an important bearing on
how he painted or wrote. It is the rationale also of our
political imagination: a politician's "credibility" is measured not so much in terms of his past performance as
through a reading of what sort of personality he "projects."

But it is in an increasingly passive spirit that we
take self-disclosure to be a moral good; this passivity is
forced upon us by the very nature of our belief. An existence of unrelieved confession, openness, and revelation of
inner secrets would be absolute hell. It is by no accident
that encounter groups are pleasurable only as weekend affairs at hotels, nor that in marriages sustained confrontation leads so often to divorce, nor that the political imagination searches only for glimpses of the man behind the

Copyright © 1976 by Partisan Review, Inc.

legislator to measure the credibility of the legislator at
work. If in general people can bear only so much truth, it
would seem that they have an especially limited tolerance
when it comes to sustained awareness of the maelstrom of
envy, kindness, rapacious desire, and gentleness of which
the human psyche is composed. Most societies confine this
chaos in public forms like religious rituals or acts of obe-
dience to secular ideology, which offer alternative modes of
expression to the display of raw psychic energy. When a culture moralizes the very existence of this energy, it ensures
that its experience of the moral life will occur only in
fits and starts. The weight of circumstance, of getting
from day to day, will make the moments of self-exposure sudden upheavals beneath the surface of everyday order. The
upheaval people do not so much greet with demonic glee as
humbly accept, for when you are under the whip of primal
passion you are forced into heresy for real.

It is true that a life of constant psychic disguise
would be as intolerable as a life of constant self-revelation. All cultures arrange some rhythm of alternation between the two; the question is how people feel the rhythm:
do they believe there is equal value in moments of disguise
and revelation, or are people unmoved by the virtues of conventional, ritual behavior and aroused only when self-dis-
play occurs? This question of the value placed on self-revelation is a social and historical question; the seriousness
with which people take their psyches depends on the culture
in which they live. It is important to keep these dimensions of the question in mind, for all too often the critics
of authenticity, after paying lip service to the conditions
of advanced capitalism and of secularism which have led
people to be so concerned with their private feelings, cast
aside the social considerations and criticize authenticity
as an abstract psychological condition. Instead of being
regarded as a product of a deformed culture, the desire for
authenticity comes to be seen as a sign of the innate sin-
fulness of human nature. This is the failing of Theodor
Adorno's The Language of Authenticity, for example. His
critique of authenticity soon puts the reader on familiar
conservative terrain; the impulse life of man comes to be
equated per se with the destructiveness of self-revelation;
therefore social repression per se becomes a moral good.
One of the great virtues of Lionel Trilling's Sincerity and
Authenticity, which is conservatism of an altogether different and more noble kind, is to show how the morality of authenticity is ineluctably the product of historical changes
in modern culture. Moreover, Trilling has shown how the emphasis on self-revelation which erupted in the last decade
is not a freak condition whose origins lie simply in the war

between the generations in the late 1960s; this self-absorp-
is the result of hidden changes in modern culture in the
making since the French Revolution.

Self-revelation is also social, rather than an abstract
psychological, preoccupation, for the attitudes people have
about their own emotions they tend to project on others.
People feel close, and their relationship seems real, if
they show themselves to each other; by contrast, it is hard
for us to imagine that people determined to hold things back
in each other's presence can have much of a relationship.
An authentic social relationship must thus progress through
mutual self-revelation; inauthenticity in social relationships is identified with what used to be called discretion.
The ideal, authentic social bond is today alluded to in
many familiar code words that posit a society in which
people are "open" to each other, "responsive to each other's
needs," ready to "interact freely." All of these code words
convert social relationships into psychological transactions;
the model underlying all of them is a bizarre form of canasta
in which each of the players competes to show the others the
cards of identity he holds.

There is a technical sociological word whose changing
meaning captures this conversion of social relations into
psychological terms: it is Gemeinschaft. The sociologist
Ferdinand Tönnies at the end of the nineteenth century used
the word to mean full and open emotional relations with
others. In opposing Gemeinschaft to Gesellschaft he wanted
to create an historical, rather than a purely analytic contrast. Gemeinschaft relations existed in the precapitalist,
preurbanized world of the ancien régime; gesellschaft relations, in which people split up their emotions according to
the principle of the division of labor, Tönnies depicted as
characteristic of the modern world. Much as he mourned the
loss of gemeinschaft relations, he never thought they could
be revived, for that would mean reviving the hierarchic, personalistic world of the ancien régime. The longing for
Gemeinschaft he in fact criticized as "displaced pastoral-
ism."
Today, Gemeinschaft has been redefined, shorn of the
historical meaning Tönnies gave it, and converted into a
moral absolute--a condition of authenticity, of good faith.
The celebration of Gemeinschaft as a pure state is captured
in the ordinary English translation of the word: community.
When people are open with each other and expose their feelings to each other, they create a community. An encounter
group is the most obvious example of a community conducted
on psychological principles of openness, butthese principles
enter into ideas about other kinds of communities as well.

In the debates about centralization and decentralization in
urban planning, for instance, the proponents of decentralization often argue that local communities should take pre-
cedence over the needs of the city as a whole, because in
the local community people have real human relationships,
in which they can be open with each other, get to know each
other, and share their feelings, while strangers in the city
at large don't. And this notion of community is connected
with disclosure: thus, in the literature on the family as
a community, full interaction is often presented as an optimum condition, and the insistence on one's right to keep
things back from those one loves is seen as a form of bad
faith which threatens the family as a whole.

Needless to say, the authentic interchange, the authenticity event, is only infrequently experienced. Local communities do have occasional flashes of this feeling of
people really sharing with each other--usually during periods of crisis when the community is threatened from outside. But micro-communities (and these would include the
family) can bear moments of mutual self-disclosure only as
periodic upheavals below the surface of day-to-day order.
Yet no matter how infrequently we can actually experience
Gemeinschaft, we persistently seek it out, measuring real
social relations by this ideal which can be sustained only
in imagination. What I want to show here is why the very
idea of self-disclosure, the authenticity event, the open
community, is destructive. This ideal makes our real social
relations seem sterile, and often poisons human relationships by creating a sense of crisis which can be resolved
only if the persons involved abandon each other. My critique does not assert that Gemeinschaft is destructive per
se, but attempts to indicate why changes in modern society
have made it so. These changes involve the redefinition of
nineteenth-century eroticism into twentieth-century sexuality, and the transformation of privacy as it was understood
in the last century into a new idea of intimacy.

Eroticism Transformed Into Sexuality

When we think of our great-grandparents' experiences of
physical love, we are most likely to think about the inhibitions and repressions. Victorian bourgeois prudery was so
extreme it occasionally acquired an almost surreal quality;
a common practice, for instance, was to cover the legs of
grand pianos with leggings, because a bare leg as such was
thought "provocative." This prudery lay at the root of a
number of psychopathologies especially acute at the time--
not only hysterias, but also what the Victorians called
"complaints," which among women were manifested by such

symptoms as uncontrollable vomiting at the sight of menstrual blood and among men by such symptoms as acute attacks of anxiety after the discovery of an ejaculation occurring during sleep. Certainly no one today could possibly hope for a return to such repression. Yet it is important to see the rationale behind this sexual repression and even to comprehend a certain dignity among bourgeois men and women in these Puritanical struggles with themselves. A code of eroticism ruled nineteenth-century bourgeois consciousness, an eroticism composed of three elements.

The first of these elements was the belief that states of feelings and signs of character manifest themselves involuntarily. Hence, what is deeply felt or deeply rooted in character is beyond the power of the will to shape or hide: emotion appears unbidden, and at moments of vulnerability emotion is a betrayal. The involuntary expression of emotion received its greatest theoretical elaboration in Charles Darwin's The Expression of Emotion in Animals and Man. Darwin connected the involuntary betrayal of emotion with the necessities of biology which ruled the human organism. But the same idea had more popular expressions which sought to indicate ways of detecting transitory states of feeling. Thus, depression was supposed to reveal itself by involuntary tension in the cheeks, an episode of masturbation by the sudden growth of a spot of hair on the palms.

Similarly, character traits were to be read through details of appearance. The involuntary expression of character involved a particular system of cognition, as in the practice of phrenology and Bertillion measurement: the shape of the skull, hand, or foot supposedly revealing the presence of certain characterological traits which the criminal, defective, or salacious person could do nothing to disguise. The Bertillion measures of criminality concern millimeters of difference between the cranial shape of the criminal and the law-abider. Because these involuntary clues of personality were like cameos, personality itself was felt to be so difficult to control; one might control most of one's behavior and still some little thing would give one away.

In such a culture, anxiety about sexual matters formed part of a larger belief that the expression of all feeling escaped control by the ego. One's only defenses were either to shield oneself as completely as possible, to neutralize one's appearance, as the Victorians did through their clothing, or to attempt to repress feeling itself. For if a transitory emotion is uncontrollably manifest through the most minute clues, one can be secure only if one tries to stop feeling in the first place. Shielding and denial, then,

are logical consequences of believing in the <u>immanence</u> of
the personality; the line between inside and outside is dis-
solved.

This Victorian belief led to a fetishism of appearances.
I use this term more in a Marxian than a Freudian sense, to
indicate how the trivia of appearance could be believed to
be signs of a whole human being. If the self speaks through
minutiae of appearance, then every appearance must be a
guide to some characterological state. Thus, it becomes
logical to cover the legs of a piano with skirts, because
an exposed leg is the sign of lewdness. In the clothing of
the Victorian era, this fetishism of appearances was especially strong. A gentleman wearing a drab black broadcloth
coat could be distinguished from an ordinary bourgeois wearing a similar garment because the buttons on the gentleman's
sleeve could actually button and unbutton. For men this
fetishism centered around questions of class; for women it
centered around sexual propriety. The differences between
the dress of "loose" women and the proper ladies who appeared in <u>Le Moniteur de la Mode</u> lay in minor distinctions
in the use of color for shawls and hoods, or the length or
shortness of gloves. Minute differences between objects
speak of vast differences in feeling between those who wear
them.

In the sections of the first volume of <u>Das Capital</u>
where Marx takes up the subject of fetishized objects, he
explains them as a veil modern capitalism draws over production relations, so that the inequities of production,
which might be visible if goods were conceived of simply in
terms of use, are obscured; these objects seem instead to
contain mysterious and enticing psychological qualities.
Missing in his analysis, however, is a consideration of the
psychological consequences of becoming mystified, of believing in the minutiae of man-made things as personality omens,
for the person so mystified. The Victorian bourgeoisie was
more than a class laboring under an illusion; it was also a
class trying to make sense of its daily experience on the
basis of this illusion. People scanned the public world
for signs of the private life of others at the same time
that each attempted to shield himself from being so read.
This double process of searching and shielding was hardly a
simple state of equilibrium or a matter of balance between
public and private.

Sexual relations in a world conceived in such terms had
of necessity to be social relations. Today, having an af-
fair with another person would not be likely to cause someone to call into question his or her capacities as a parent,

or--if it were someone sufficiently "liberated"--his or her
capacities as husband or wife. For the Victorian bourgeoisie,
those connections had to be made. If every act, every feeling, counts in terms of defining the whole person, then emotional experience in one domain carries unavoidable implications about the character of the person acting in another.
A violation of morality in one sphere signifies a moral violation in every other; an adultress cannot be a loving mother,
she has betrayed her children in taking a lover, and so on.
Again, I wish to call attention not so much to how brutal
this repressive code could be as to the premise which produced the repression. The immanence of character in all
appearances forced the Victorian to weigh each experience in
relation to other experiences to us seemingly quite dissociated. For all the desire to flee the world at large and
hide in privatized, isolated places, the Victorians had to
measure the acts of the private sphere on the basis of their
public implications. This is how a system of social relations was produced.

People so concerned with the involuntary expression of
feelings, with fetishized objects, each of which contains
clues to the personality of its wearer or owner, people who
conceived of their sexual relations as having repercussions
beyond the bedroom door; these people inhabited an erotic
world. It was a sensual world, but overwhelmingly, uncontrollably so, and as a consequence it prompted attempts at
repression and self-discipline which were in fact of the
most destructive sort. Eroticism and repression: these two
psychological phenomena dominated the capitalist bourgeoisie
in its first epoch of domination in Western society.

What has occurred in the present century is that we have
overturned the eroticism of that world, hoping to escape
from its repressiveness, in such a way that we have substi-
tuted a new slavery for the old. We have desocialized physical love, turning eroticism into the more isolated and inward terms of sexuality. But this change is not so much a
contrast as it is a form of continuity with the Victorian
situation. The desocializing of physical love which has
taken place in the present century is a result of carrying
to an extreme the Victorian's first principle, the principle
of personality immanent in appearances.

Now it is a truism that Americans and American culture
tend to be personalistic in their view of social relations.
Aspects of class, race, and history are easily abandoned in
favor of explanations of events which center on the character and motivation of the participants involved. But the
American viewpoint represents a psychological vision of

society which is taking hold in Western Europe in the present century as well. Think, for instance, of how Left leaders in England, France, and West Germany are spoken of as "legitimate" or "credible." Such judgments are based not so much on the leader's ideological purity or coherence as on his ability to appeal personally and so to command the votes of those who do not share his left-wing ideas. Or think of the increasing tendency of people in the upper working classes and the new classes moyennes to view their positions in society as simply the result (or failure) of their personal abilities. This personalizing of class occurs even though people may understand in the abstract that their positions result from the blind workings of advanced capitalism.

To view one's experience in the world as a consequence or mirror of one's personality is narcissism. By this is not meant love of self, but more precisely the tendency to regard the world as a mirror of self. When personality is believed to be causally at work in all human experiences, the world will soon seem to be only a mirror of the self. At this point, the idea of Gemeinschaft acquires its absolutist, moralistic form: if people are not revealing their inner feelings to others, they are not being "for real." As the principle of immanent personality appearing in the nineteenth century has expanded its hold upon people's minds to such an extent that all appearances in society seem real only as manifestations of personality and personal feelings, narcissism has been mobilized as a cultural condition. Narcissism has become the norm, the code of meaning.

As we know, the psychological disorders which psychotherapists treated most often eighty years ago were hysterias. But today hysteria is a relatively rare complaint. Instead, what appears most commonly in clinics for treatment are "character disorders." The patient feels empty, dead, or dissociated from the people around him, but has no objectified neurotic signs such as an hysteria or a phobia. One has this feeling of deadness, of an inability to feel or to relate to other people, precisely because one has begun to conceive of that outside world as a peculiar mirror of self. It exists to fulfill the self; there are no "human objects" or object relations with a reality all their own. The peculiarity and the destructiveness of this narcissistic vision is that the environment of the human being becomes less fulfilling the more it is judged in terms of its congruence with or subservience to self needs. Expectations of the outside grow enormous. It is a sea in which the self floats without differentiation; and for the very reason that expectation of fulfillment becomes at once so vast, and so amorphous, the possibilities of fulfillment are diminished. Be-

cause there are no boundaries between self and others, experiences lose their form; they never seem to have an end or
a definition of completion. Concrete experience with other
people therefore never seems "enough." And because gratification from this oceanic, boundaryless outside never seems
enough, the self feels empty and dead. The obvious content
of a character disorder is, "I am not feeling;" the hidden
narcissistic content is, "the world is failing me, and so I
am not feeling."

This shift in clinical data from Freud's generation to
the present has occurred because the society has changed.
It is a society which has orchestrated the energies of narcissism around the theme of emotional "liberation." This
new music drowns out the very idea of society itself. By
"society" I mean a situation in which people weigh different
domains of experience against one another so that choices
are made, and people sacrifice one set of gratifications for
the sake of another. Moreover, "society" involves the operation of external, believable constraints upon the self (like
class consciousness, religious commitment, manners or rituals
of kindness) having a reality of their own.

Let me give an example of how this mobilization of narcissism operates in one of the popular ideologies of sexual
liberation. In Germaine Greer's The Female Eunuch one is
presented with a clear and incontestable picture of the domination of men over women in jobs, education, homelife, etc.
Then one is told that this situation obtains because a social "system" operates in society: men aren't tyrants, modern life simply makes them play that role. Well and good.
The next step in the argument is the assertion that a woman
has to rebel against this system by being able to do anything a man does; she "deserves" whatever men have. The
author argues that women should try to get "total gratification," that they deserve whatever they desire. As the book
unfolds, the idea recedes that a system of bad social relations created female oppression in the first place. A woman
who gets what she "deserves" in the system simply changes
positions in the game of musical chairs. Thus, in the
course of making an argument for the equality of the sexes,
Greer winds up forgetting about society. Total gratification of the self becomes the alternative to systematic dis-
crimination against females. The world, at first seen as
socially unjust, becomes a mirror or resource for the self.
This is the unfolding of narcissism at work in an ideology
of liberation, and it defeats goals of that ideology by
gradually blotting out the reality which caused the problem.
The conversion of the desire for social liberation into the
desire for personal liberation maintains the system as a

whole; the social network of inequalities is not challenged, although the sex of a few of the players may be changed.

But what is truly perverse about narcissistic projections is that they are seldom self-evident; nor are they simple demands for pleasure. For example, one attempts to explain to himself why he has failed to be upwardly mobile, and arrives at the conclusion--despite all his abstract knowledge that social organization controls his chances--that some personal failing is the cause. In this he is mirroring the self onto the world. This is as much a narcissistic formulation as is the credo that in the end liberation from a subdominant role involves free gratification of the self through use of the "resources" of society.

Elsewhere I have argued that there is a correlation between the increasing bureaucratization of modern capitalism and the mobilization of narcissism in society. Large-scale bureaucratic structures function according to a system of promised rewards based on the supposed talent, personal affability, and moral character of the employee at work. Reward thus becomes tied to the exercise of personal ability, and the failure to receive reward--in fact a systematic necessity since large bureaucracies are sharp pyramids--is increasingly interpreted by those in the lower middle positions as a failure on their own parts to be rewardable, by virtue of their personalities. Thus, it is also for functional reasons, and not only as a consequence of the intensified belief in personality manifest in all social relations, that narcissism has come increasingly to be mobilized.

When bureaucracy and the collective consciousness of personality join forces, it becomes possible to believe, as the Victorian bourgeoisie could not, in a protean self. The American psychiatrist Robert J. Lifton defines a protean self as a conception of identity involving the belief that one's personality is always undergoing fundamental changes, or is capable of doing so. There is consequently no core of "innate" human nature or of fixed social conditions which define it: it is a self so totally immanent in the world that it is a product of immediate appearances and of sensations. This notion of selfhood puts an immense premium on "direct" experiences with other people; it detests reserve or masks behind which other people are felt to lurk, because in being distant they seem to be inauthentic, failing to take the immediate moment of human contact as an absolute. About this protean self, Lifton is highly ambivalent. He sees its value, as a pure analytic construct, because the vision of an infinitely malleable human nature does away with the whole problem of ahistorical, innate personality

factors; but he fears this protean man somewhat as a cultural phenomenon. For if one dedicates oneself so thorough-
ly to a life of direct sensate experience, one cannot make
long-term commitments, and resistance to immediate moments
which are malign or unjust becomes difficult. A protean man
may live a rich immediate life, but only at the cost of
accommodation to his environment. By contrast, the person
who feels his selfhood to be constant has acquired the will
to resist his environment.

Belief in a protean self follows logically from a loss
of boundaries around the self. If the world of impersonal
necessity is erased, and reality becomes a matter of feeling,
then changes in feeling, transitory impressions and sensations come to seem like fundamental changes in character.
The self-concept as a whole is thus fetishized, just as
individual objects were a century ago.

This totally phenomenological view of the self achieved
one of its most dramatic expressions in the commune movements of North America and Western Europe during the last
decade. These communes were seen less as arrangements valuable or pleasurable in themselves than as models of how the
larger society ought to reform itself. Indeed, the millenarian commune involves a conviction that changes in one's
immediate life space are so important and changes in the
quality of feelings between people who become intimate are
of such value, that these changes somehow become emblems of
what the whole of society ought to be like. Thus, there is
no vision of the operation of society as something different
from intimate transactions. But it is possible to believe
that changes in one's immediate feelings are political in
character only if one assumes that the whole of society is
made up of creatures defined essentially by their immediate
feelings. And if one accepts such an assumption, then it is
logical to believe that this society of protean selves is
waiting for a "model" of changes in feeling to guide the
transformation of the whole.

But the "counter culture" here is only an expression of
the larger ordinary culture as is evident in the realm of
sexuality. In this area, belief in a protean self suggests
to people that "who" they are depends on who their lovers
are: love thus becomes another mirror of the self. In the
last century, Lamartine could put forward as a poetic conceit the notion that "who I am depends on whom I love today,"
but that conceit has been transformed in this century into a
commonplace. And as a result of the acceptance of this notion, sexuality has been burdened with tasks of self-definition and self-summary which are inappropriate to the physical

act of making love with another person.

There are many studies of the anxiety with which people approach the matter of sexual selection of a partner, and some evidence that this anxiety has replaced the rather different anxieties of two generations ago about the experience in bed the partners might later have. If the act of lovemaking itself has lost its terror, the prior selection of partners seems to have absorbed that same terror. For all the talk in the popular media about promiscuity, there is little evidence that free-floating sexuality is on the rise. Rather the reverse; "mate-selection" (as the sociologists call it) seems to be becoming a tense process because the choosing of someone to sleep with is a reflexive act: it tells who you are. Thus, in the Van Burgh researches, for example, there appears a consistent worry about whether "this person is right for me," a worry which crowds out such questions as "is he or she attractive?" or "do I like him or her?" Once the self becomes a protean phenomenon, the reality of the other person is erased as an Other; he or she becomes another "resource" for inner development, and loving the other person for his or her differences recedes before a desire to find in that person a definition of oneself.

The belief in protean selfhood treats intimate interchanges like a market of self-revelations. You interact with others according to how much you tell them about yourself; the more confessions you have made, the more "intimate" you have become. When the partners are out of self-revelations, the relationship all too often comes to an end: there is nothing more to say. Making human contact by marketing confessions in this way easily results in boredom, or it forces people to start all over again in a relationship once they have shown themselves to each other. Thus, psychologists, for instance, usually have to start over when training as diagnostic interviewers. The tyro interviewer is convinced that to treat another human being with respect, he must match whatever is revealed to him with a similar experience of his own. This shows that he "understands," that he "sympathizes." In fact, this card game leads neither to understanding nor sympathy; if he is any good, the trainee starts over with the knowledge that real respect for other human beings involves a respect for human differences. Such a therapist is increasingly in a minority, however, as the marketing of self-revelation appears in encounter groups, "T" groups, and the like. The marketing of confession has also become one of the main modes of interaction through which married people experience short-term extramarital affairs, which are initiated by that classic complaint, "my spouse doesn't understand me." The market exchange of confession

has a particular logic in a society ruled by the fear that
one has no self until one tells another person about it: and
this is the protean man's dilemma.

These are the three conditions of modern personality: it
is narcissistic, protean, and marketable. Together these
conditions color our imagination of social relations which
are real, authentic, and moral: there is an insistence that
these relations also be open--people must show themselves to
each other; they must tell the truth, about themselves, and
about the strengths and weaknesses they perceive in others,
no matter what. Such psychological imagination of authentic
social life represents a notion of <u>Gemeinschaft</u> stripped of
all the historical associations Tönnies first gave the word,
and converted into a moral absolute. This notion of <u>Gemein-
schaft</u> is not only crude and uncivilized, but also, as a
moral interpretation of human relations, as an expectation of
what reality ought to be, it has enormous destructive power.

One of the destructive aspects of modern <u>Gemeinschaft</u>
lies in the way it perverts the experience of conflict. It
makes people see conflict as an all-or-nothing contest for
personal legitimacy. If you are different from someone else,
and he reacts negatively when you reveal yourself to him, the
conflict appears to you to challenge the very worth of yourself. Once conflict is escalated to the point at which it
becomes a question whether it is legitimate to have your own
feelings, only two endings are possible: one can either try
to overwhelm the other person so that he is no longer different, or one can abandon him. Either way, an ongoing human
relationship is destroyed. An unavoidable difference challenges the narcissistic modality of seeing the self mirrored
in the world. This mode depends on projection and the sharing of similarity. In conflict, people are faced with a
problem which will not mirror each in the other, which cannot be marketed to the other. The experience of interpersonal
conflict then escalates to the more all-encompassing question
of which person, which side of the difference, should legit-
imately exist at all.

Just as individuals involved in such a conflict struggle
over who they are rather than specifically what they want,
larger groups view conflict as a form of struggle for legitimacy between collective personality types. Instead of a
neighborhood, class, or ethnic group pressing for specific
gains, it tries to find an "identity." It then uses this
identity as a moral weapon: because the group has a collective self, it therefore deserves fulfillment; because the

members of the group feel close, feel as one, their claims
upon society are legitimate, no matter what the substance of
the claims, or the means of their realization. An extreme
example of this pattern is to be found in ethnic-terrorist
groups. The fact of having discovered a common self legit-
imates the means of terror to preserve that end; and this is
equally true at the opposite end of the political spectrum
in Falangist or other modern Fascist groups. If one moves
from these political extremes to more ordinary forms of conflict, the same process is at work. The locality asserts the
integrity of its demands against a central planning organization not on the grounds that the actual practices of the
central bureaucracy are unjust but rather on the grounds that
the solidarity of the neighborhood will be destroyed. It is
no accident that local politics conducted on this basis of
identity-as-legitimacy so often becomes self-defeating. At
the same time as the neighborhood fights the outside world
for threatening its solidarity, within itself it conducts
continual tests of who really belongs, who really expresses
the sense and the interests of the collective whole, and this
testing leads to fragmentation, intramural struggles over who
is an authentic member of the group, and so on. Powerlessness comes from the very attempts to define a collective
identity instead of defining the common interests of a diverse group of people. This latter idea was I believe what
Marx meant by a class out for itself, an idea Gemeinschaft
obliterates.

What makes Gemeinschaft pernicious is that this desire to
share one's feelings with others like oneself feels so close
to the ideal of fraternity. It would be unreal to deny the
general human need for fraternity, but what has happened today is that the concrete experience of fraternity has become
perverted by the assumptions about personality which rule
our culture. Fraternity should be a condition of common action, and its psychological rewards ought to come from pursuing action together. Today, fraternity is regarded instead
as a state of being--one in which finding out who we are becomes of overwhelming concern. And the very process of defining who we are, like the process of defining a single me,
is troubled because conflict, diversity, and complexity are
not part of the process of self-definition. When conditions
of external or internal conflict face the group, unity of impulse becomes more important than concrete common interests.
If there is not unity of impulse (and, given the richness of
human impulses this is rare), then the struggle centers on
the question of whose impulses are legitimate. Marriages or
long-term affairs become testing grounds of personalities,
rather than relationships with constraints and interests of
their own. Larger communities break apart along the same

lines: no matter what the scale of modern <u>Gemeinschaft</u>, the logic of sharing feelings is that the self is made powerless when feelings cannot be shared. This is why there exists the conviction, now so prevalent, that one's real problems are those of the arousal of feeling in the presence of others. Sometimes this problem is overtly presented as self-failure; but covertly, in collective as well as individual cases, the desire for <u>Gemeinschaft</u> with others is really an accusation against the world for not mirroring back to one the resources for completing an identity.

I have spoken of a crisis of legitimation produced in ordinary life by our very belief in being open and psychologically "liberated." Jürgen Habermas takes up this theme in more abstract terms in his influential book, <u>Legitimations-probleme in Spatkapitalismus</u> (The Problems of Legitimation in Late Capitalism). In this work, Habermas calls for a better society in which human communication is freed of all the constraints of arbitrary power which operate in advanced capitalism. He advances a theory of cognition <u>(Erkenntnisleiten-den)</u> in which "distortion-free" communication between people is possible. I think his view is psychologically naive but also instructive. For Habermas, the psychological world is deformed by the social realities of power and control; while Habermas seems to be talking about the pressures of capitalism, his real worry, I think, is about the intrusion of society itself upon psychological openness, for in any society power of an unjust and dominating sort will exist. The problem of modern culture lies in its assumption that human beings must somehow get away from the issue of domination in order to be communicative and open. To dream of a world in which psychological processes of open communication, processes which are taken to be morally good, are free from social questions, is to dream of a collective escape from social relations themselves. The elevation of a psychology of openness above the dirt and compromise of power politics is precisely the dynamics of modern <u>Gemeinschaft</u>. Habermas's work is not so much a critique of the problem of legitimation now faced by the culture as the very embodiment of this problem.

In sum, the repressive eroticism of the nineteenth-century bourgeoisie was the product of three beliefs. The first and most important was that individual personality was immanent in appearances in the public world. The second was that all the details of appearance had a personalistic meaning, so that appearances became fetishized. And the third was that, for all the desire to retreat and make private the realm of feeling, intimate emotions like those involved in sex remained exposed and judged in societal terms. There are also

three beliefs underlying modern Gemeinschaft. The first is
the intensification of the idea of immanent personality to
such an extent that the world becomes a narcissistic mirror
of the self. The second is the belief that the self is a
protean phenomenon. The third is that this immanent, protean self interacts with others and creates the conviction
of its own existence by engaging in market transactions of
self-revelation. In part, then, twentieth-century personality is clearly a consequence of nineteenth-century assumptions, but it is also significant that modern terms of personality coincide with the increasing bureaucratization of
industrial society. And the result of modern Gemeinschaft is
that people unable to "find themselves" become all-too-will-
ing to abandon each other.

Privacy Transformed Into Intimacy

Today the phrase "the private family" seems to connote a
single idea, but until the eighteenth century privacy was
not associated with family or intimate life, but rather with
secrecy and governmental privilege. There have been numerous
attempts to explain the union of privacy and family life in
the modern period, the most notable and direct being that of
Engels. Because of the sterility of human relations in the
productive system of capitalism, Engels argued, people concentrated their desires for full emotional relations in a
single sphere, the home, and tried to make this sphere privileged, exempt from the emptiness which pervaded office or
factory. Engel's idea of privatization supplements the movement which Tönnies perceived in the larger society from
Gemeinschaft to Gesellshaft relations; in sum, the family
becomes a miniature Gemeinschaft in a largely alien world.

The term privatization has become a cliche' today among
those who study and write about the family, and has taken on
two overtones which obscure its meaning. All too often writings on the private family (an isolated nuclear family in
form) assume that privatization can actually work: people who
want to go and hide can really do so. This is the assumption of the historian Phillippe Ariès and those of his school
when they talk about the family withdrawing from the world
in modern times. Missing in this account is a recognition
that the social forces which divide work from family also in-
vade the family itself. If we do recognize the pervasive
power of capitalism, then we must think of the experience of
privatization in the nineteenth-century family as an attempt
to make the family warm and snug against the outside, but an
attempt which constantly failed because the alien world or-

ganized personal relations within the house as much as impersonal relations without.

Secondly, the cliché of privatization misleads by suggesting a static condition that of a permanently privatized
family. But what happens once the family becomes privatized?
After all, this process of privatization has been at work
for 200 years, and yet many of those who study it use terms
to describe it which apply to fixed emotional states: "isolation," "emotional over-involvement with kin," and the like.
Surely the families of Emma Bovary, Buddenbrooks, and Herzog,
all ostensibly privatized, are not the same.

Let us return for a moment to Engels's view of the pressures creating privatization in the nineteenth century.
These are pressures of displacement in one direction: from a
work experience more and more empty to family experience
forced to provide a full range of emotional relationships,
including those which properly belong to, but have been
shifted from, the public world of production. What then
would generate a contrary pressure, so that the family ultimately failed in its efforts to provide a refuge, failed to
become securely privatized? Critical in producing this contrary motion was the idea of personality revealed in external
appearances which had crystallized by the 1860s and early
1870s.

In the child-rearing manuals published in the 1860s in
both France and England, a common, almost monotonous theme
occurs: for children to grow up with stable characters, they
must maintain orderly appearances in the family circle. Not
only must the child, whether boy or girl, act consistently
through "good habits" and "beneficent rules," but the parents
must display good habits and act consistently in front of
their children. The reason this advice about family dynamics was given is that the Victorian bourgeoisie feared that
if appearances were not routinized in the home, and if spontaneity were not effectively suppressed, then the personality
would never crystallize and the child would never grow emotionally strong. This fear is linked to a series of assumptions which we have already examined; since basic personality
traits are linked even to the minutiae of external appearances, in order for basic personality traits to be formed
appearances must be rigidly controlled.

For all the desire family members had to withdraw from
the terrors of the world into a relaxed warm zone, the codes
of personality in the last century pushed family relations
back into the welter of contradictory impulses of order and
immanence which troubled the public world. Between husbands

and wives the same pressure for stabilization of behavior existed as governed the relations of parents and children. Love between man and woman depended on the ability of the partners to conform to the rules of what a husband and wife should be. But if adherence to rules of propriety was necessary at home, the realms of work and home were not therefore identical. In the home, changed appearances would threaten the partners' trust in each other, threaten their sense that each knew who the other was. A repressive, rigid routine became the means of certifying that the marriage itself was real--just as the child was thought to grow in a healthy way only if he experienced others in terms he could trust. For the Victorians, trust meant trust to remain the same.

Thus, the privatization the family experienced in the nineteenth century was a consequence of its search for an order in which stable personality could flourish; and yet it involved a belief in immanent personality which thrust the family back out into the very anxieties about order and immanent meaning which ruled public life. Both the desire to retreat and the reconstruction of the outer society are elements of privatization. The first would soon have exhausted itself as a desire had not the second so insistently thrust family dynamics back into the public contradiction, so that the family's mission of orderly retreat never seemed accomplished.

For families of the present generation, privatization on these terms has ceased to exist. There is no longer a world alien to the self to which the self refers. For example, to preserve a marriage as a social contract, people today are not willing to observe proprieties of the rigid sort which characterized the last century; if one is obliged to make great sacrifices of immediate feeling and perception about the other partner in the marriage, then the marriage itself soon seems sour. Because so many nineteenth-century people were imprisoned in respectable but loveless marriages the breaking of rigid codes of correct behavior may well seem all to the good. The problem is that this change in the terms of privatization has not liberated individuals within the family, but paradoxically, has made the family bond more important and more destructive. The reason for this is that when family relations become withdrawals from the world the person has no experiences outside the family which can be used to judge experiences within it. The family comes to seem the terrain on which all emotions are displayed: emotions which are not familial have no reality because the world outside is only instrumental. The movement from privacy to intimacy is a movement from the family as an un-

successful private institution to the family as a tyrannical,
psychologically pure universe.

What is the rationale for conceiving of the family as
socially withdrawn and emotionally complete? It is that of
the narcissistic mirror. If the family is not a work unit as
in the ancien regime, if it is not an arrangement involving
an arbitrarily rigid set of roles, as in the nineteenth century, then what appears in this "free" psychic network has a
reality and purity unsullied by alien contingencies. Once
freed from the world, the family will appear to be a disclosure of pure psychological experience. The lessons of such
experience will then be taken out beyond the family circle,
and psychological transactions in the world will be judged
in terms of familial categories, which seem like pure types.

Let me give some concrete examples. Patterns of friendship among adults at work today follow a course unlike those
which obtained four generations ago. The more a friendship
between adults at work grows, the more attempts are made to
integrate the adults into the respective family circles and
to form friendships between the families. American middle-
class workers open the gates to the home rather readily to
their friends, the French bourgeoisie rather reluctantly, but
the path of friendship is the same. One of my students has
done a comparative study of friendships between middle-class
adults in London and Paris in the 1870s, as these are por-
trayed in the pulp fiction of the time, and found something
entirely different from this modern pattern. Among males, a
friend became someone with whom you could engage in escape
from the rigors of the family; a friend was someone to take
out rather than invite in. Among females, friendship also
involved progressive dissociation from family relations; a
friend was someone who could become a confidante for griev-
ances against both one's children and one's spouse. Because
women were incarcerated in the house, female relationships
appeared familial, but in fact friends in the house provided
a chance to rail against the tyrannies of the home. A century ago, then, friendship for both sexes meant escape from
family ties; today it involves a reinforcement for them.

Take even something so apparently opposed to the mores
of the bourgeois family as the hippie commune. A study of
communes in the 1960s found them to be insistently concerned
with reliving old family issues and relationships in order
to create a higher kind of family. A common problem for the
collective family arose whenever psychological needs were
asserted against the whole, such as the need for psychological experience outside the commune. When these needs could
not be made consonant with the commune's life, then the com-

mune was threatened. For example, if you are sleeping with
someone not part of the commune, why is it you don't ask him
or her to come live in the commune? The refusal to familize
these relations was taken as a betrayal.

    The most profound indicator of the family as an image of
a purely psychological and morally dominant condition comes
from the realm of ideology. Today our concept of psychological emancipation involves liberation of the self rather
than liberation from the self. In ordinary speech we ideal-
ize being able to express our feelings openly or feeling free
to do so. Habermas's model of open communication has its
vulgar counterpart in the belief that social institutions are
bad at the moment when they get in the way of human expression. One example of that vulgar belief is Germaine Greer's
Female Eunuch. Liberation of one's feelings is basically a
familistic ideal. Liberation from one's feelings is a non-
familistic ideal. The first refers to the possibility of experience in which anything one wants, any sensation one has,
can be received by others; that is, liberation of one's feelings presupposes an accepting environment, one in which interest in whatever one does feel, and appreciation for it,
will be shown by others. The model for such an accepting environment is the child displaying himself to an audience of
adoring parents. Liberation from one's feelings, on the
other hand, refers to the possibility of experience which is
impersonal, experience in which the person observes a convention, plays a role, participates in a form; the classic locus
of such liberation is the city, its classic name cosmopoli-
tanism.

    But the contrast cuts further. The self-conscious dis-
play of newly discovered feelings to an accepting environment is usually a post-Oedipal phenomenon--that is, it follows upon the child's first consistent declarations of his
own independence. The display of behavior in which the child
participates in a social form with impersonal conventions is
usually a pre-Oedipal experience--it follows upon the child's
discovery that he can engage in games. Game-play involves
pleasure of a form, a convention not dependent upon indivi-
dualized, momentary impulse. Conservative critics of the
modern culture of a boundaryless self usually base their attacks on the notion that this culture is regressive and
childish. The real problem is that the terms of modern bourgeois personality are not regressive enough; these terms do
not permit the adult to call upon the most fundamental and
earliest of the social impulses, the impulse to play. The
reproach one ought to make to the notion of liberation of the
self is that these energies of play remain dormant as the
adult regresses only to that point where the self-conscious

declaration of his own feelings was an event his protector-parents accepted, even cherished. It is this most fragile, withdrawn moment of family history which becomes enshrined as a cultural ideal when we dream of free self-expression.

A society in which liberation of self replaces liberation from the self as an ideal has obliterated any possibilities of self--transcendence from its moral life. Instead of transcending the self, one makes it into a comprehensive standard of reality. One does not balance public against private; instead, one assumes that one is, that life is authentic, when one focuses inward, taking moments of self-disclosure in the family to be the reality in which the self is nourished. The outside is vaguely threatening but also simply vague, a reality of necessities, constraints upon the self, bonds to be broken. It is this intimate imagination which destroys the idea of self-transcendence; and when that idea is destroyed, the moral life of a society has become fully secularized.

Transcendence of the self is so deeply a part of the Catholic and Protestant traditions that it is easy to imagine that this ideal is possible only in an overtly and strongly religious culture. But that need not be so; any society believes in transcendence when people imagine that their impulse life may be destructive as well as constructive, and therefore create social rituals or conventions which served to control the impulsive destructiveness of the people in the society. Two of the least religious thinkers of modern times, Rousseau and Freud, believed in their very different ways in a society where such transcendence becomes a moral goal. It is true that ideals of transcendence do involve a certain kind of faith, if not in collective progress or the moral regeneration of man, at least in the possibility of people collectively lifting some of their own psychological burdens.

It is this faith which a society destroys when it sees only personality immanent in any genuine human relationship. The immanent is opposed to the transcendent, the intimate to the social; an anxious expectation of self-gratification is opposed to a faith in mankind despite itself. I believe that this secular vision of ours is a blindness. If a society believes in the unqualified liberation of the self, how can it take into account the simple fact that human beings have destructive impulses which should be hidden from others? This is why a society like ours, celebrating the sheer existence of human feeling, cannot be called privatized. There is no understanding of what it means to harbor an impulse in private. There is no understanding of what disguise to be only a further proof of the authoritarian injustices of present social arrangements; we are prone to convert discretion and tact into signs of domination. Surely the word liberation is itself misleading as a description of the present situation if it connotes a state of progress. A hundred years ago, personality was socialized only by ideas of repression; today it is not socialized at all. These are opposite and equal evils.

Today there is community without society: this pure Gemeinschaft is a self-destructive ideal which reifies the family and makes us blind to the evil in ourselves. We might try to end this destructive Gemeinschaft from within or from without. The best element of the women's movement has tried the first course; people start with their own immediate feelings and through group transactions and common action try to socialize these feelings, to move from a language of intimate injuries to a shared political commitment. When this process works, men as such cease to be the enemy and the set of conditions which lead men to play oppressive roles comes into focus; a social reality comes alive. One of the great failures of the antiwar movement of the last decades, by contrast, was its inability to organize discontent among soldiers because many people in the antiwar movement so personalized the war that every soldier was treated as responsible for the war unless he somehow could prove himself innocent. The idea of the woman's movement that intimate relations can be transformed into social relations is based on the notion that the destructive features of Gemeinschaft can be eliminated if people resolve truly to understand the origins of their feelings.

Destruction of Gemeinschaft from within is obviously a difficult business: chancy in its outcome, perhaps too idealistic in its assumptions, certainly dependent on considerable character strengths for the people involved. The other strategy against this modern Gemeinschaft is no less difficult. To weaken Gemeinschaft from without would mean renovating an impersonal social world in which people could escape their families or the burdens of their own feelings. The classic terrain of such a social world is the cosmopolitan city. Yet how can one revive crowd life, a social existence passed among relative strangers at bars, theaters, and cafes, when all the pressures of the culture are oriented to restoring human scale, creating environments in which people get to know each other as individuals and other forms of oppressive localism? Or when the city itself is fled as a place of danger, dirt, Negroes; when the logic of capital investment in the city follows the cultural logic of withdrawal? No one could argue that the city in its present state is very attractive, nor that the flâneurs of Baudelaires

Paris or the sense of the <u>monde</u> of Marivaux's can be re-created as though city planning were an essay in nostalgia. Yet the only concrete strategy against the psychological morality of modern capitalism, the only countervailing power from without against destructive <u>Gemeinschaft</u>, lies in renovating the city as a human settlement. The word crisis is abused but it has a meaning: there is a moral crisis in advanced capitalism and there is an urban crisis in it; these two have a real relationship, for until we learn how to create a living, impersonal environment in which people can wear the masks of sociability, and so disguise themselves, the pursuit of a true, essential, and authentic self will continue to be our moral compulsion.

About the Author

M. Brewster Smith is professor of psychology at Steven-son College, University of California at Santa Cruz, and president of the American Psychological Association for 1978. He is the former editor of Journal of Social Issues *and* Journal of Abnormal and Social Psychology *and the author of* Humanizing Social Psychology *(Jossey-Bass, 1974).*

3

Encounter Groups and Humanistic Psychology

M. Brewster Smith

From one angle of regard, this symposium is retrospective, a requiem for a social movement of the '60's that is well past its peak. In California, the traffic from San Francisco down Route 1 to Big Sur has declined, and in the programs that continue at Esalen, encounter groups dissolve into an ever new mix of bodily and spiritual disciplines and delights. From a more inclusive perspective, however, the ecological niche that encounter groups occupied for a while in contemporary American culture is still there, a persistently aching void that a parade of successor movements, some touchingly innocent, some crassly commercial, vie with one another to fill. The void seems never to get filled, and the social, psychological, professional, ethical, and maybe religious problems raised by the encounter group movement are still very much with us.

My discussion of encounter groups and humanistic psychology must therefore attend also to the broader "human potential movement" of which encounter groups formed a central part, and to the still more inclusive half-world of somewhat therapies and somewhat mysticisms into which it shades off without clear boundaries. With respect to humanistic psychology, I will likewise need a dual referent: to the humanistic psychology movement with which encounter groups and "growth centers" became identified, and to a conception of humanism in psychology that the movement has seemed to me largely to desert.

In this necessarily cursory venture, I am acutely aware of the lack of the kind of data that could contribute to a more solidly based understanding of the role of encounter groups in recent social change. We now have some information about the effects of encounter groups on participating individuals--measurable effects that are by no means spectacular (1). We have no good information, so far as I know, about

57

the shifting clientele of seekers for intensive group exper-
ience--their social characteristics, their motives, their
hopes and expectations, their movement among alternative pro-
viders of packaged love, communion and human meaning--or
about the heterogeneous company of leaders, facilitators, and
gurus, some from within the established mental health professions, most probably not, who offer these commodities (2).
So our consideration of encounter groups as a social move-
ment--in the longer run, probably the most interesting aspect
in which to view them--has to be essentially speculative.

Two Views of Encounter Groups

A good starting point is provided by two quotations that
put before us the widely divergent value-laden appraisals
with which encounter groups have been greeted. The first is
from Carl Rogers, one of the founders of humanistic psychology as a movement and, in his earlier years, a staunch and
imaginative innovator in bringing scientific methods to bear
upon the fragile interchanges of counseling and psychotherapy. The second is from Sigmund Koch, initially an experimental psychologist, then an integrator and critic of systematic scientific psychology, still later a humanist in
psychology who has been caustically critical of the preten-
sions of psychological science and of most claimants to the
humanistic label.

In a very personal book commending encounter groups to
the public as "one of the exciting developments of our time,"
Rogers wrote that "the encounter group or intensive group
experience . . . is, I believe, one of our most successful
modern inventions for dealing with the feeling of unreality,
of impersonality, and of distance and separation that exists
in so many people of our culture" (3).

But then hear Koch: "It is my assessment that the group
movement is the most extreme excursion thus far of man's
talent for reducing, distorting, evading and vulgarizing his
own reality. . . . It is adept at the image-making maneuver
of evading human reality in the very process of seeking to
discover and enhance it. It seeks to court spontaneity and
authenticity by artifice; to combat instrumentalism instru-
mentally; to provide access to experience by reducing it to
a packaged commodity; to engineer autonomy by group pressure;
to liberate individuality by group shaping. Within the lexi-
con of its concepts and methods, openness becomes transpar-
ency; love, caring and sharing become a barter of 'reinforce-
ments' or perhaps mutual ego-titillation; aesthetic recepti-
vity or immediacy becomes 'sensory awareness.' It can provide only a grotesque simulacrum of every noble quality it

courts. It provides, in effect, a convenient psychic whore-
house for the purchase of a gamut of well-advertised existential 'goodies': authenticity, freedom, wholeness, flexi-
bility, community, love, joy. One enters for such liberating
consummations but settles for psychic strip-tease" (4). In
the 'encounter game,' says Koch, "The essential complexity,
indeed ambiguity, of the meanings of human actions and expressions, thus of personhood, is damped out" (5).

The two quotations capture the main hopes and claims for
encounter groups and similar intensive group experiences--
and the main criticisms (strongly stated) from a standpoint
that is humanistic in the traditional sense. They provide a
frame for the evaluative consideration of encounter groups as
a social movement. They anchor extremes of evaluation that
run a gamut between hailing encounter groups as a solution to
Modern Man's vulnerability to loneliness and despair, through
regarding them as mostly harmless and sometimes helpful sub-
stitutes for the grand-right-and-left mixers of an earlier
day, to decrying them as shallow and meretricious eroders of
personal and interpersonal integrity.

I don't think there is much argument about the general
cultural situation to which the encounter group movement is
responsive. Phrasings will differ, but Carl Rogers' way of
putting it does very well: "the feeling of unreality, of
impersonality, and of distance and separation that exists in
so many people of our culture." It is our special version
of the modern predicament initiated by the collapse of reli-
giously based tradition and the erosion of Gemeinschaft, a
predicament heightened for recent Americans by the decisive
break with history in a nuclear and electronic age, by our
national entanglement in a demoralizing war, by the assassi-
nation of our most hope-inspiring leaders, by the undermining
of former bases for hope and commitment as the previously un-
challenged doctrine of unending growth and progress becomes
visibly untenable. As the practicing humanist Robert Penn
Warren has written, "any true self is not only the result of
a vital relation with a community but is also a development
in time, and if there is no past there can be no self (6).
Since our ties to community in time have been strained and
attenuated, our age has not been friendly to integral, well-
rooted selfhood.

The Humanistic Psychology Movement

In order to be in a position to discuss the involvement
of the encounter group movement with humanistic psychology, I
need first to review the background of the humanistic movement in American psychology, a revolt against the positivistic

behaviorism that by midcentury had long dominated academic
psychology and also a revolt against psychoanalysis (7),
which provided a major theoretical basis for the rapid postwar growth of clinical psychology. There had long been a
minor current of "abnormal and social psychology" that co-
existed uncomfortably with the mainstream of positivistic
experimental psychology. Out of this current emerged the
psychology of personality in the late 1930's, under the leadership of such major figures as Allport and Murray, soon to
be joined by Murphy, Maslow, Kelly, Rogers, and May (8).

All of the eminent psychologists just named, together
with Charlotte Bühler (9) who while still in Vienna had
launched the study of lives in life-span perspective, met
with various other psychologists and humanists in a conference at Old Saybrook, Connecticut, in 1964 that formally
launched the humanistic psychology movement as a "Third
Force" distinct from the then regnant forces of behaviorism
and psychoanalysis: a movement to bring psychology back to
concern with human experience, values, and choices; to
counteract the alienating stream of mechanism in psychology;
to balance the concern with pathology that characterized the
emerging field of clinical psychology with a focus on positive human potentialities for love, creativity, and fulfillment (10). While apostles of the European philosophical
currents of existentialism and phenomenology were among the
group, it is important to recognize that it also included
the entire academic leadership of personality theory, apart
from strict Freudians, in what (in retrospect) now appears
to have been its great period.

What began as a movement within psychology was soon
swept by forces characteristic of the 1960's into a tra-
jectory that carried it out of contact with the academic
science. The older academic leaders dropped out, and of the
triumvirate--Rogers, Maslow, and May--to whom the movement
looked for intellectual leadership, at least Maslow and May
became profoundly ambivalent about the irrationality and
kookiness perpetrated in the name of humanistic psychology
(11). How did this happen? In effect, encounter groups and
allied therapies captured the humanistic psychology movement.

Michael Murphy and Richard Price had started the Esalen
Institute in 1962 (12), drawing on strands examined by our
chairman-editor (13) from sensitivity training, Gestalt
therapy (14), and the mystical disciplines. At about the
same time, the two major modes of cultural alienation so
attractive to youth in the '60's both made their appearance
in California: the counter-culture (15) of the flower-
children and drug-oriented hippies with its passive

withdrawal, and the New Left of the Free Speech Movement at Berkeley and progressively more chaotic campus protest (16)-- respectively postures of copping out or lashing out in relation to the "square," conventional social order that to many no longer afforded a setting for hope and commitment.

The mid-sixties also witnessed a further flowering of the "sexual revolution," when for the first time since the 1920's major shifts apparently took place in patterns of sexual behavior away from the traditional double standard and toward an increasing acceptance of casual as well as relational sex by females as well as males (17). Therapy fads proliferated, communes were established (18), mystical cults spread and the charismatic movement with its strange penchant for "speaking with tongues" penetrated the established churches (19).

So, even when encounter groups were at their height, they were hardly a separate movement, an isolatable phenomenon. They were rather, as Rosabeth Kanter says of communes, part of "a more general culture of spiritual, therapeutic, and communal seekership in the United States, creating a demand for short-term personal growth experiences in temporary communities (20).

The "Culture of Seekership"

This "culture of seekership," which informed the encounter group and human potential movement and engulfed humanistic psychology, can be described in terms of interrelated themes. I will tag them with the following labels: individualism, human perfectability, self-disclosure, emphasis on the "here and now," hedonism, and irrationalism (21).

Individualism

For all its emphasis on the intensive group experience, the encounter movement and humanistic psychology in general has been radically individualistic, a respect in which it resonates with a dominant theme in American culture at large. The group is put to service to save individual souls. The center of value is found in the fulfillment of the individual, virtually stripped of interdependence and commitments to other lives. What has been called "the new narcissism" (22) has emerged. Thus Maslow's conception of self-actualization as the acme of personal growth (23). Thus the hippie's careless tolerance of "doing one's own thing"; thus Fritz Perls' Gestalt prayer to feel responsible only for one's own life,

not to be one's brother's keeper. Thus the transitory character of intense relations in the weekend encounter group or
in unstable "intentional communities."

The experience of self-dissolution in communion is indeed sought, but as an experience, a transcendental high,
rather than as a confirmation of hardly earned and commit-
ting relations between real and complex people. The "transpersonal psychology" that has been widely touted as the creative front of the humanistic movement amounts to an eclectic
melange of the old mysticisms under psychological auspices
(24): individual finite selfhood is taken as an inferior
state to be transcended, but it is transcended in a mystical
(and individual) experience of merging with the All, not in
concrete and caring relations with finite others.

Human Perfectability

A doctrine of human perfectability runs through most
writings in humanistic psychology, and distinguishes them
from the somberness of Freud. Rollo May, whose strong roots
in European existentialism lead him to attend to the tragic
aspects of life, is the major exception (25). For Rogers,
Maslow, and many lesser figures, the prevailing doctrine is
watered-down Rousseau: Man is essentially good, and his good
qualities will predictably unfold and blossom if only properly nurtured. It is a romantic or--better--a sentimental doctrine that predisposes those who hold it to neglect realistic
considerations of politics and ethics, which are concerned
with how to enhance actual life among imperfect creatures who
are often at cross-purposes with themselves and others.

In the encounter and human potential movement as such,
the assumption of perfectability promotes seekership, and
when it is combined with the equally American faith in instrumental gimmicks and prescriptions, the unattractive and
superficial features, the manipulative features held up for
scorn by Koch appear. Such an easy, such a delusory route to
growth and perfection! Koch complains and I agree. But it
is a route that has many precedents in our past, whether in
the revivals, camp meetings, and faith healing of an earlier
day or the Moral Rearmament sessions of Susan and God a generation ago. A further problem with the doctrine of perfectability is that it breeds dissatisfaction with the imperfect
relationships possible in the real world--with real marriages
and families, for instance--and does not sustain the patient
effort that is required to make them better or to make them
last.

Self-Disclosure

Still another common theme is the high value set on self-disclosure--the "transparent self" (26)--for its own sake and as a near panacea for the troubles of the soul. Conventional reserve and the artificialities of politeness and civility are rejected as hypocritical; the thing is to "let it all hang out." Nakedness, both literal and symbolic, is idealized, and not just for sexual reasons. In a society that lacks the device of tu-toyer to distinguish intimate relationships, first-naming, symbolizing a readiness for intimacy, seems to be carried by the young to the point of serious inconvenience. The undoubted reassurance and healing that can come in a truly intimate relationship from sharing what is guiltily or troublesomely private is taken as a universal principle, leading to a general unconcern for the protection that privacy can give to vulnerable individuality. In loving personal relationships, intimate sharing is protected by the mutual attachment and care of the partners. In professional helping or therapeutic relationships, intimacy is shielded by the safeguards of professional ethics. Not so in encounter groups, or in the quick and easy self-disclosure of the culture being described. When intimacy is so readily claimed and granted, it gets cheapened. Supposed intimacy becomes less truly intimate. The promiscuously transparent self is at risk of becoming less a self.

The "Here and Now"

Emphasis on the "here and now" is shared by the encounter movement and Gestalt therapy; as a college teacher it seems to me to have characterized virtually a whole generation of youth and to pose very difficult obstacles to education. Deliberate narrowing of time perspective surely has its therapeutic uses, especially with people who are "hung up" on inhibitions and scruples carried over inappropriately from a different past. Zimbardo has illustrated the process involved: a narrowed time perspective releases impulsivity (27). There are obviously occasions when this is appropriate and desirable. And there are many when it is not.

Self-control and commitments to self and others only make sense in a longer time frame; self-respect, loving care, and planfulness can emerge only in lives that are linked to a past and a future. (We are reminded of what Robert Penn Warren had to say about the conditions of well-rooted selfhood.) Total immersion in the "here and now" strikes me as a tactic of the hopeless, akin to the fatalism of the culture of poverty (28). It is a stance that helps one tolerate

bleak realities that one does not feel one can do anything
about. Unfortunately, living in the moment may also exclude
coping with realities that had better be faced.

Hedonism

The hedonism that runs through many byways of humanistic
psychology, from sensual massage and sensory awareness training to "gut feel" as the criterion for ethical choice, is obviously related to life in the "here and now" with minimal
baggage of human or moral commitments--and thus with minimal
sense of identity. "If it feels good, do it." Hendin, a
psychiatrist to youth, holds that the search for sensation
follows from a basic estrangement from one's feelings, in
which the desire to keep all options open reflects emptiness,
not inner freedom; in which people out of touch with their
feelings (and likeminded social scientists, I would add) come
to think of life as wholly a matter of playing roles or even
games (29). (Transactional Analysis--TA--with its game metaphors merges with Gestalt therapy as the most popular way of
theorizing about encounter groups.)

Hendin, too, sees the root problem as one of hopelessness,
and writes as follows:

> Increasingly what unites people in this culture is a
> sense of shared misfortune and depression, a feeling of
> impotence in the face of forces they feel they cannot
> shape or control. Erikson put it sensitively when he
> wrote that "any span of the [life] cycle lived without
> vigorous meaning, at the beginning, at the middle, or
> at the end, endangers the sense of life and the meaning
> of death in all whose life stages are involved."
> Erikson pulls back from confronting the forces today
> which endanger meaning. But we are a culture in which
> the elderly are treated as refuse, the middle-aged in
> their discontent turn to the young for salvation and in
> so doing undermine youth by expecting the impossible
> from them. (p. 334).
> The flight from emotion seems the only available way
> out in a culture where people are increasingly adrift
> in their discontent. (p. 339).

Irrationalism

Irrationalism completes the thematic package. Irrationalism is reflected in disrespect for intellectual content in
the group process--"mind-fucking," Fritz Perls called it; in
the affinity of humanistic psychology for the occult (belief

in the firm factuality of E.S.P. is taken for granted among humanistic psychologists as a matter of course); in reliance on intuition over evidence; in disparaging rational problem solving; and in the debased level of intellectual discourse in much that passes as theoretical writing in humanistic psychology and its associated therapies. Frankel has written eloquently about the inherently self-defeating aspect of irrationalism in the counter-cultural movement, saying, in effect, that the irrationalist inhabits a dream world in which reality imposes no obdurate limitations and people never have to resolve cross-purposes--for rationality is simply the hard-earned strategy and tactics of dealing with a difficult, limiting reality (30).

Instrumental rationality has obviously been abused, particularly in the linear, technological thinking, supposedly value-free, that has become especially identified with the defense establishment. It is true that attempted rationality has not been working very well for us. It is also true that the requirements of life and work in a bureaucratized, technological society have underplayed the life of feeling; have given, by an old metaphor, head one-sided priority over heart, or, by a newer one, left-brain thinking unbalanced predominance over right-brain thinking. Correctives and re-balancing are in order. But the pendulum swing against well-considered rational thought, as exhibited in the encounter group movement and humanistic psychology, is destructive rather than corrective unless still further correction is applied to it.

Current Manifestations

The encounter group movement has peaked and is in decline, but the culture of seekership as just sketched continues unabated. And the successors and competitors of encounter are no improvement. In particular, est (Erhard Seminars Training), last year's fad that may already be making its exit along with the more benign TM (transcendental meditation) as a general panacea, is an ominous phenomenon, the more so because it has received the enthusiastic endorsement of much of the leadership of the humanistic psychology movement including Michael Murphy, the co-founder of Esalen. est is flagrantly individualistic, its purpose and claim being to make Pawns in De Charms' sense into Origins of personal causation (31). It is unabashedly commercial and drastically manipulative, drawing for its marathon sessions on strong techniques of self-reconstitution previously used in Synanon on hardcore addicts and by communist "brainwashers" on ordinary citizens (32). It may well be effective--though

its effects have not been measured. But what sort of "humanism" is it for a packaged venture in "human potential" to
soften up its audience by browbeating them as "ass-holes,"
by stretching their endurance of bladder tension, by fati-
guing them to the edges of toleration? To the extent that
this is clever applied psychology (and clever it appears to
be (33)), it is a menacing development, and an insult to the
idea of humanism.

It is surely a sign of the present disarray of the human
potential movement that Robert Ornstein, whose Psychology of
Consciousness legitimized the esoteric psychologies of human
potential for many, now feels compelled to inveigh against
the false prophets with their profits (34). But he continues
to hold forth the Sufi mysticism of Indries Shah as a truer
gospel.

Where, then, are we? It is easy to decry the mindless-
ness of the encounter group movement and its successors. In
doing so, I come out sounding much like Sigmund Koch. But it
is necessary to take the movement seriously, for what it
tells us about the serious lacks in our way of life that generated it. The movement did not solve our problems. All the
same, attention to it may help us see more clearly what these
problems are.

Underlying Social Lacks

Harking back for a closer look at themes touched on earlier, I see three interrelated lacks to which the encounter
movement was responsive. These lacks, which can be thought
of as different facets of the same complex problem, are de-
ficits in community, in meaning, and in hope.

Deficit in Community

The encounter movement sought to meet the deficit in
community by superficial communion, by ersatz "communitas"
(35) among transparent selves. It sought to give quick
gratification to lonely, rootless people's needs to feel
accepted and loved. The lack that we suffer from is not so
easily to be satisfied. Real steps toward solution, if they
are possible for us at all, will come in the social and political realm, in the reconstruction of the world of work and
school and family, of neighborhood and recreation. Our lack
makes us vulnerable to pseudo-solutions, which may be shoddy
and mindless and could become fascistic. At least in our
psychological theories we should be wary of giving further
support to the predominant extremely individualistic values

that undermine community. We need to bring human interdependence into better focus. The requirements of meeting our compounded ecological crises could help to foster such a fundamental reorientation.

Deficit in Meaning

The deficit in meaning is the familiar modern lack to which existential philosophy, Jungian psychology, and even modern psychoanalysis (36) is responsive, as is the proliferation of occult and mystical doctrine at the boundaries of the encounter movement. It is by no means firmly established that people as self-conscious creatures can live without the supernatural frame of meaning traditionally provided by myth, ritual, and religion: we have tried doing without it for so short a time, and not done well. It seems unlikely that people can live well without some frame of transcendant values. Perhaps the current popularity of cults and the occult foreshadows a new religious age, a dark age in terms of the Enlightenment values of science. Or perhaps we can work out a drama of significant purposes in more human terms. Whatever the outcome, I hope we can do better than the amalgam of psychology and mysticism that passes as "transpersonal psychology." Psychology can learn much from religious disciplines and symbolism, but when it tries to be religion, it is shoddy, superficial religion and bad psychology.

Deficit in Hope

The deficit in hope to which the encounter movement and humanistic psychology responded with hedonistic fixation on the "here-and-now" seems, as I have already suggested, the most plausible reason for the timing of the movement, and I therefore look on it as potentially the most remediable. Paradoxically, I am somewhat hopeful about our hopelessness, since the '60's and '70's thus far have been filled with such an unusual array of special events and circumstances that evoked hopelessness and cynicism. Given new national leadership that begins to face some of our difficult real problems, hope can regenerate, and with it the readiness of youth to make commitments, to reach back to the past and contemplate a desired future that is worth the effort. True, the problems of our country in the contemporary world may be beyond satisfactory solution. But hope, which to me is the primary human virtue and resource, is not the same as optimism. We can struggle hopefully with exceedingly difficult problems if we can select and maintain effective political and moral leadership.

Whither Humanistic Psychology?

So much for some lessons from the encounter movement concerning problems of our society and culture. What about the humanistic psychology that the movement captured and deflected? I think we need to start over again, more or less where its founders left off.

The need for a psychology respectful of human values is still inadequately met. But developments in scientific psychology in the meantime have reduced the gap between the assumptions of psychological science and the requirements of a humanistic psychology. The old dogmatic positivism that dictated the shape of a behavioristic science is largely discredited; contemporary mainstream psychology is far more open and tolerant of diversity in subject matter and method than the psychology against which the humanistic movement rebelled. At the center of the current mainstream is a cognitive psychology—a fact that would have astonished Watson and Hull, and still astonishes Skinner—which remains a kind of behaviorism but begins to deal with recognizably human processes of thinking, imaging, and remembering without the dogmatic exclusions of the old positivism. True, mainstream psychology has yet to deal adequately with the life of feeling. But a humanistic psychology no longer needs the same firm barriers against science that it once felt necessary to defend itself against the claims of scientism, which denied its right to exist (37). As mainstream science in psychology has become less monolithic and less anti-humanistic in its claims, there is less occasion, or excuse, for humanistic psychology to be anti-scientific.

We need a humanistic psychology that can talk coherently about feelings and about such matters as community, meaning, and hope; that can deal with the phenomena of selfhood and human interdependence in historical context. Such a psychology needs to take the emotional and irrational, the mystical, the transcendant into account. If in its own conceptual structure it can avoid the mistake of <u>being</u> emotional and irrational, mystical, or religious, there is no reason why it cannot join an open array of psychological sciences.

References and Notes

1. See, for instance, M. Lieberman, I. Yalom, and M. Miles, <u>Encounter Groups: First Facts</u> (Basic Books, New York, 1973); P.R. Kilmann and W.M. Sotile, <u>Psychol. Bull</u>. <u>83</u>, 827 (1976).
2. For a comprehensive but rather uncritical survey of this range of activity, see <u>The Intensive Group</u>

Experience, M. Rosenbaum and A. Snadowsky, Eds. (Free Press, New York, 1976).

3. C. Rogers, On Encounter Groups (Harrow Books, Harper & Row, New York, 1973), p. 127.

4. S. Koch, Amer. Scholar Autumn 1973, 639.

5. Ibid., 651.

6. R.P. Warren, Democracy and Poetry (Harvard Univ. Press, Cambridge, Mass., 1975).

7. Recent psychoanalytic scholars have sought to disentangle the humanistic strands of Freud's clinical formulations from the mechanistic assumptions of his "metapsychology." See R.R. Holt in Psychoanalysis and Contemporary Science, R.R. Holt and E. Peterfreund, Eds. (Macmillan, New York, 1972).

8. G.W. Allport, Personality: A Psychological Interpretation (Holt, New York, 1937); H.A. Murray, Explorations in Personality (Oxford Univ. Press, New York, 1938); G. Murphy, Personality: A Biosocial Approach to Origins and Structure (Harper, New York, 1947); A.H. Maslow, Motivation and Personality (Harper, New York, 1954); G. Kelly, The Psychology of Personal Constructs (Norton, New York, 1955); C. Rogers, On Becoming a Person (Houghton-Mifflin, Boston, 1961); R. May, Existential Psychology (Random House, New York, 1961).

9. C. Bühler, Der menschliche Lebenslauf als psychologisches Problem (S. Hirzel, Leipzig, 1933).

10. For an account of the conference see R. May in Edited Transcript, AHP Theory Conference (Assoc. for Humanistic Psychol., San Francisco, 1975), p. 4.

11. Personal communications.

12. C. Tomkins, The New Yorker 5 Jan. 1976, 30.

13. K.W. Back, Beyond Words: The Story of Sensitivity Training and the Encounter Movement (Russell Sage Fndn., New York, 1972).

14. F.S. Perls, R.E. Hefferline, and P. Goodman, Gestalt Therapy (Julian Press, New York, 1951).

15. T. Roszak, The Making of a Counter Culture (Doubleday Anchor, Garden City, 1968).

16. K. Keniston, Radicals and Militants: An Annotated Bibliography of Empirical Research on Campus Unrest (Lexington Books, D.H. Heath, Lexington, Mass., 1973).

17. C. Chilman, Adolescent Sexuality (National Institute of Child Health and Human Development, Washington, D.C., in press).

18. R.M. Kanter, Commitment and Community (Harvard Univ. Press, Cambridge, Mass., 1972).

19. See especially The New Religious Consciousness, R.N. Bellah and C.Y. Glock, Eds. (Univ. of California Press, Berkeley, 1976); D.E. Harrell, All Things are Possible:

The Healing and Charismatic Revivals in Modern America
(Indiana Univ. Press, Bloomington, 1976).

20. R.M. Kanter in _The Intensive Group Experience_, M. Rosen-
    baum and A. Snadowsky, Eds. (Free Press, New York, 1976),
    p. 148.

21. The topic has been so much discussed from so many per-
    spectives that it is pointless--and impossible--to iden-
    tify source references for these ideas.

22. P. Marin, _Harpers_ Oct. 1975, 45.

23. M.B. Smith, _J. Humanistic Psychol._ _13_, 17 (1973).

24. See _Transpersonal Psychologies_, C.T. Tart, Ed. (New York:
    Harper & Row, 1975).

25. R. May, _Love and Will_ (Norton, New York, 1969).

26. S.M. Jourard, _The Transparent Self_ (Van Nostrand, New
    York, ed. 2, 1971).

27. P. Zimbardo in _Nebraska Symposium on Motivation 1969_,
    W.J. Arnold and D. Levine, Eds. (Univ. of Nebraska Press,
    Lincoln, 1970).

28. M.B. Smith, _Social Psychology and Human Values_ (Aldine,
    Chicago, 1969), p. 210.

29. C. Hendin, _The Age of Sensation_ (Norton, New York, 1975).

30. C. Frankel, _Science_ _180_, 927 (1973).

31. R. DeCharms, _Personal Causation_ (Academic Press, New
    York, 1968).

32. T.R. Sarbin and N. Adler, _Psychoanalytic Rev._ _57_, 599
    (1970-71).

33. S. Fenwick, _Getting It: The Psychology of est_ (Lippin-
    cott, New York, 1976).

34. R.E. Ornstein, _The Psychology of Consciousness_ (Viking,
    New York, 1972); _The Mind Field_ (Grossman/Viking, New
    York, 1976).

35. V. Turner, _The Ritual Process_ (Aldine, Chicago, 1969).

36. A. Wheelis, _The Quest for Identity_ (Norton, New York,
    1958).

37. I. Chein, _The Science of Behavior and the Image of Man_
    (Basic Books, New York, 1972).

Bernard G. Rosenthal is a research consultant in psychology and a member of the Department of Psychology at Mundelein College. He has written over 35 papers in psychology and social psychology, particularly group behavior, and is the author of The Images of Man *(Basic Books, 1971). Dr. Rosenthal is currently working on a book concerning social and environmental conditions for the optimization of behavior.*

4

Encounter Groups: Some Empirical Issues, Explanations, and Values

Bernard G. Rosenthal

This paper deals not only with the ideology, values and related societal aspects of encounter groups but also, in brief counterpoint, with some of the empirical evidence that place the idealistic rhetoric of the movement in factual, if abbreviated, compass.

In the psychological pantheon of claims made by the encounter group movement can be found the following prospective graces: an open and unimpeded orientation to sensation and feeling; the search and affirmation of genuine personal identity; the effort to achieve interpersonal understanding through the acceptance of the feelings of one's self and others as well as through the dissolution of interpersonal ritual and hypocrisy; the elimination of intellectual defensiveness as a barrier to emotional insight and mutual understanding; the liberation of affirmative sexual impulse; the achievement of a richer awareness of one's affective potentialities, inner experiences, and esthetic, sensory, and proprioceptive impulses; and the prospective establishment of a benign small-group community of interpersonal felicity and candor as well as of diversity and robustness in the expression of opinion and in decision-making processes.

Empirical Issues

But aside from the hopes and visions that attend the encounter ideology, what, in hard fact, has been the upshot of encounter experiences so far as they have been investigated? Other scholars (5, 15, 24) have given exhaustive summaries of this issue and, though not presently aspiring to their level of comprehensive review, you will forgive me if, for the sake of continuity of the argument of this paper, I present only a hypercapsule summary, in balance I hope, of such empirical assessments as have been made of the alleged enhancing effects of encounter groups and, also, of their detrimental outcomes.

One of the difficulties in making an assessment of the alleged effects of encounter experiences is that the amount of change reported appears to vary with the source of the judgments. The trainee's opinion of the effectiveness of his behavioral change tends to be far more optimistic than that of observers. For example: Miles (22) reported that of 34 high school principals who had participated in NTL programs, 82 percent indicated improved functioning subsequent to their training. Ratings by their "back-home" colleagues, however, indicated that only 30 percent had undergone changes. The fact that the participant's own responses are more enthusiastic than those of his associates was also found by Taylor (30). More recently, Lieberman, Yalom, and Miles (17) report that peers of group participants believe that only about half as many of the latter experience positive change as a result of encounter experiences as do the participants themselves or as do the leaders of their groups.

Indeed findings must always be interpreted with the utmost caution in this area, in view of the crucial methodological problems involved. For instance, aside from the factors just mentioned, interpretation of judges' ratings of group participants are difficult to assess in that peers tend to assign less change to colleagues who complete a group training experience than do either their superiors or subordinates. Compounding the difficulty of interpreting the rater's judgments is the fact that many studies are based on opinions obtained at the conclusion of the training period. In the absence of a pre-training baseline the results are of questionable value. In addition to these factors must be added the as yet unascertainable effect of experimenter bias, i.e., the curious phenomenon that those investigators favorably disposed to encounter groups and often their avid practitioners seem to obtain more benign and positive outcomes in their studies (1, 2, 3, 23, 25) than those who may be thought to be less enamored of 'encounter' philosophy and practice (9, 10, 19).

Besides the issue of response bias, there are at least two other methodological problems which further limit the value of many studes. (1) There are often no control groups to aid in assessing the impact of techniques, leader personality, style, level of training, length of meeting time, and other such variables. (2) The measures used have frequently been global rather than specific. Under these circumstances, it is not possible to determine the specific nature of the changes experienced--e.g., interpersonal sensitivity, empathy, warmth, objectivity, and other such presumed goals of the encounter groups. Indeed, in those studies (4, 11, 12, 17) where measures directed to specific feelings, behaviors and traits are used, the results are far less encouraging than in those (1, 2, 23, 25) where global measures are employed.

Other studies permit us to conclude only that most of the clients who choose to respond to the inquiries of their former group leaders report that they "gained something" from the experience. But there is no evidence that those who did not respond to such requests for information also 'gained something'. In view of the fact that almost one-fourth or more of group participants in previous studies (23, 25) offered no information whatsoever on the effects of their experiences, a balanced conclusion on this matter is unreachable and it may not be beyond the bounds of legitimate conjecture to suggest, in view of comparable survey research in other behavioral areas, that the effects of these 'encounters' for non-respondents may not have been as salutary as those reported by responding participants.

Parloff (24) to whose detailed review of this literature up to 1970 I am vastly indebted in compiling substantial portions of my own mini-resume, prudently concludes his discussion of these matters as follows:

"Participants in encounter groups report favorable reactions and are frequently described by others as showing improved interpersonal skills. The evidence is meager that such participants undergo significant attitude or personality change, and evidence that group training improves organizational efficiency is not compelling. What is clearest is that these groups provide an intensive affective experience for many participants" (24, p.19).

In a comprehensive summary and appraisal of the more recent research literature (from 1973 on), it can be adduced from the condensed tables that Lieberman(15) presents in this paper that of nine pertinent investigations the effects of encounter groups, either studied independently or in comparison with other group approaches (including placebo treatments), the encounter group mode was enhancing or more effective in four instances but in the other five reports showed no demonstrable salutary improvement or no greater and, indeed, sometimes even less positive effect than other group orientations. On methodological grounds, Lieberman finds much to criticize in these more recent studies: "More important, the particular change conditions are usually unspecified. The fact that such groups work best with 'volunteer subjects', i.e. people who seek such settings ordinarily with positive expectation of change, leads one to question the

robustness of these findings. The fact that individuals less
able to be changed are also those whose values are less con-
gruent with the particular set espoused by such groups casts
doubt on the meaningfulness of the findings" (15, p.225).

Even within the compass of the encounter group orientation, it appears that the nature of the leadership style may
have a significant effect on the participants' outcomes or
their risks of psychological casualty. Thus, in a study by
Lieberman et al (18), it was found that a 'provider' type of
leadership, as defined by these investigators, is associated
with a positive change of 57% of participants whereas "managerial" types of leadership is associated with 0% positive
change. Similarly, with regard to risk of psychiatric
casualty, negative change and dropout, a "provider" leadership style shows the lowest risk factor and those of "ener-
gizers" and "impersonals" the highest.

In addition, there is the intriguing finding that some
studies of placebo group treatments hint at the prospect that
factors other than those uniquely associated with the encounter mode itself may, in possibility, be responsible for
such enhancing effects as have been obtained in some encounter group studies. In the McCardel and Murray (20) report,
for example, these placebo conditions were recreational activities and relatively non-intensive interactive events that
embodied indeterminate factors which produced high changes
comparable to those obtained from other orientations including that of three encounter groups, and in the McLeish and
Park study (21) those placebo treatments which yielded
equally positive results as other group orientations merely
consisted of groups of S's who were observing participants
engaged in human relations training.

If, then, the evidence of benign, liberated and enhanced outcomes from encounter experiences is sometimes uncertain or questionable, there is some support for the con-
tention that disadvantaged effects sometimes occur. Such
consequences may be emphasized because of the quite large
size of encounter groups and seminars, which often means that
their leaders cannot pay sufficiently close attention to the
individual participants. But because most encounter procedures, if not all, involve personal experience and relationships in some depth, touching on various buried or unacknowledged complexes, energies, or fixations, they surely
require the most acute sophistication and skill, for there
can always be a risk of a damaging outcome with participants
who are too ill, immature, or in states of incipient breakdown. In their paper "Sensitivity Training: Interpersonal
'Overkill' and Other Problems" Kuehn and Crinella (13) con-

tend that at least four groups should be excluded from T
groups: psychotics, characterologic neurotics, hysterics,
and individuals in crisis. If carried out, such a recom-
mendation might well eliminate quite a sizeable--indeed
possibly a very substantial proportion--of those now involved
in these groups. Indeed, Lazarus (14) has recently written
that the number of patients who are "victims of encounter
groups is becoming so large as to constitute a new 'clinical
entity'." Further, a number of studies (9, 10, 19) have
cited compelling instances of psychotic and other severely
disturbed reactions to encounter group exposure. In the four
groups comprising these studies, an average of 18.5% of the
participants experienced these reactions.

But, in fairness, it must also be stated that many other
investigators, among them (Mintz [23], Bach [1, 2], Rogers
[25] and Bebout and Gordon [3]) report a paucity--and often
an absence--of such severe or psycholotic reactions in their
own studies of 'encounter' effects.

As to mild and moderate emotional disturbances stemming
from these experiences, again the evidence is somewhat at
odds. In two different studies reported respectively by
Yalom et al (33) and Gottschalk (9) the incidence of these
types of disturbances was indicated as occurring in 10-15%
and 28% of their respective groups' participants. And in yet
another study, Yalom and Lieberman (32) report that 8% of the
encounter participants were psychological 'casualties',
another 8% showed some signs of negative change, and an additional 12% dropped out of these groups because of psychological reasons. On the other hand, Rogers (25), Mintz (23),
Bach (2) and Bebout and Gordon (3) report such indices vary-
ing from 0.6% to 6% in the groups they studied.

In summary, reports of mild to moderate emotional disturbances which occur during encounter group experience range
from 0.5% to 28% of the participants; negative reactions
which endure subsequent to the experience range from 0.6% to
about 18% of the participants.

Thus, it cannot be doubted, even by encounter groups
warmest adherents, that emotional disturbances--serious and
mild, transitory and enduring--can be precipitated by encounter experiences.

Beyond these issues, a number of other matters bearing
on encounter groups have been studied but since the present
paper does not pretend to be either a summary or overview of
work in this field, only immediately relevant areas of inves-
tigation will be cursorily listed together with but minuscule

elaboration of one factor that has more direct bearing on the
nexus of this symposium. For more detailed and comprehensive
reference, the reader is directed to Lieberman's excellent
critical survey (15). Among these issues bearing on the research strategies, processes and outcomes of encounter and
other 'growth' groups are the psychological matching of
leaders and clients, the experience and likeability of
leaders, the effects of tape-structured and other forms of
leaderless encounter groups as compared to leader-led groups
of similar orientation, the absence of adequate replication
of research studies, participants' traits associated with
positive and non-positive outcomes, the role of group peers
together with their personal and social values as these relate to encounter dynamics and change, and the nature of the
change mechanisms themselves. One aspect of the latter will
be very briefly touched on here. In view of the prevailing
ideology, ambience and nexus of most encounter and "group
growth" research, it surprisingly has been shown recently by
1) Freeland (7) that there is no relation between the type
and amount of feedback received and the nature of outcomes
for the group participants and by 2) Lieberman et al (18)
that absolute frequency of self-disclosure was unrelated to
outcome, "and that self-disclosure was primarily a social act
in a particular context. Self-disclosure took on salience to
outcome if some cognitive structure was constructed by the
participant around it or the meaning it had to him. -----
-- studies which isolate them (self-disclosures) as a specific mechanism have not born the expected fruit given the long
practical and theoretical interest in them. There is no
strong evidence that mechanisms such as self-disclosure and
feedback are central to the change process in and of themselves" (15, pp.242-43).

Ideological, Social
and Historical Issues

In the light of the uncertainty and inconsistency of research results bearing on the reality of encounter group processes, what can be said of the nature of the experience,
ideology, presumptive values and social implications of the
encounter movement as construed from its literature and spoken representations and from extensive and repeated first
hand observations. Further, what is the historical and
social context, and its meaning, in which the movement should
be placed.

At the outset, I would submit that the atmosphere and
conditions generating the ostensible emotional outcomes of
encounter experience represent rather a ritualization of
affect and sensitivity as well as of the practices and pro-

cedures that give rise to them. This ritualization, as I call
it, is designed to achieve an opening or heightening of consciousness. It is ritualistic in the sense that the same
proximate or possibly stereotyped procedures are almost
always used to obtain desired ends but rarely with reference
to the unique personal needs of the participants. Moreover,
it is as if the awareness and feelings desired must fit
largely into the proximate mold of liberated, spiritual, mystic, or sensually exciting affect and sensation, and profound
deviations from these modes of response or the fusion of cognitive and valuative functions with them, though not dis-
couraged, are not given much latitude to emerge. The result,
deriving from these set techniques, is a ritualization of
feeling, sensation, and interpersonal stimulation, or, in
short, an enshrinement of experiences and sensitivities that
are separated from the context of reality, cognition, and
value of everyday life.

Enshrinement inevitably ritualizes and sanctifies desired experience, and the encounter movement does so too.
There is a procedure for its evocation and a language for its
incantation and description. As part of the mysterious and
possibly magical practice necessary to achieve these particular precious, ineffable, and exotic feelings, a particular
series of rituals must be exercised (touching, seeing, kinesthetic activities, chanting, rocking, interpersonal gambits
and ploys, and so on) that distinguish these presumable humanistic experiences from those of everyday life both in the
methods of evocation and in the ends to be achieved. These
particular exotic and semireligious techniques are implemented for particular psychologic effects in much the same
way as any system of rituals, be they those of religion or of
the mechanized role-playing relationships of business and
social life that the encounter experience was designed to
remedy. Indeed, the emphasis on feelings of a certain kind
and awareness of a particular variety have in form, sanctity,
and repetitiousness much the same character as the rituals of
the everyday world, whose content, however, is of materialistic and status matters, whereas that of the encounter group
involves manufactured spontaneity, codified awareness, instant warm feelings, and elementary varieties of sensory and
affective experience.

For this diversion and escape--which is not the same as
an authentic humanism--the encounter group leader exacts the
same charge for his services as would any other expert prac-
titioner of a craft, profession, or other entertainment committed to the values of the material world. This, too, is
consistent with the ritualization and esotericism of highly
specialized professions or crafts, for they are not designed

to deal directly with the general humanistic issues of life
in the everyday world. Rather, their techniques are comparable to professional or skilled services of the role-playing,
specialized market-place society whose pre-eminent rewards
are money and status. Similarly, the service-skills of the
encounter group practitioners lie in providing diversionary
or therapeutic release valves for their clients and in per-
suading them that they are or can be spontaneous, genuinely
human, and compassionate.

May it not be true, then, that these experiences do have
the character of a ritual or of game-playing and, in effect,
often transpose the anonymous role-playing of real life into
that of instant role-playing emotion and instant personal relationships. Surely, the varnishing or advertising of self
by such warmth and congeniality is an established practice in
politics, salesmanship, and advertising and in the life of a
business society, as a whole. Is it not possible that the
encounter movement, in part, is an exercise in massive selling of the idea that humanistic, warm, spontaneous, and salutary interpersonal experiences are within reach of almost
everybody and that the encounter process is the instrument
for their attainment? If true, such a traffic in pseudo-
feeling and pseudo-humanistic experience not only may reflect
the general spirit of our advertising, selling, role-playing
culture but also may protect one from the distress of deep
self-probing and unvarnished confrontation with reality.
Thus, the picture partially emerges of a cult of ritualized
feeling and sensation, perhaps fragmentary, perhaps conjuring
up humanistic images to themselves and others to make up for
the emptiness and depersonalization of life, perhaps ardently
trying to wrest some measure of genuine humanism from their
constant emulation and play-acting at it, or perhaps anxious-
ly attempting to convince themselves and others that they are
undergoing a depth of humanistic experience. In overview,
there is a confusion between illusion and reality, between
the advertisement of a wished-for self and the real self, between the need for emulating the humanistic image and one's
real image.

Again, this is not to exclude the possibility that these
fronts or presentations of humanism do play an important personal role in a world of mechanization and exploitation.
People need to be accepted, loved, and warmed and will positively respond to the expression of those sentiments by
others. It also enhances their economic position, professional status, and interpersonal relations if they can exhi-
bit these feelings. Indeed, the salesman is an integral part
of contemporary society whether as a particular person or as
a symbol of prevailing norms. In a world of depersonaliza-

tion and conflict, what helps to effectively sell one's self or one's product is a humane and warm image.

In this sense, the encounter group is an arena for training in good contact, in facile acceptance of others and oneself, and in the techniques of compatible interaction. But these are precisely the urgencies and values of the contemporary business and professional marketplace: to get along with others, sell one's self quickly, and thereby be approved. Simultaneously, participants can experience some measure of sensory and emotional openness and fulfill other humanistic impulses as well. Thus does the encounter group movement equip its clients with those techniques of understanding, openness, and spontaneity that will ensure the greatest ease of accommodation and selling-of-self while also providing them with some degree of emotional and interpersonal fulfillment.

This does not mean, however, that the encounter group immediately and directly confronts the issues of the real world and the fundamental causes of the dehumanization in it. Rather its thrust is to build psychologic and cultural atmospheres that escape from or deny such confrontations and such consciousness. As a result, it cannot admit numerous issues of sophisticated adult dimensions of experiences to enter into its compass--hence the relatively superficial dealing with feeling and interpersonal relationships, i.e., the role-playing or ritualization of them in accordance with an unacknowledged theme of avoidance of genuinely involved, fully and deeply spectrumed interpersonal relationships and confrontations. All this, too, is abetted by the short-term nature of the encounter meetings, by a lack of concern with well-being of individual participants, which is a departure from the sacred obligation of the medicant to care for his client, and by a lack of real knowledge of the character and interest of the person(s) one shares these experiences with or of authentic contact with them as differentiated personalities.

(It should be added, parenthetically, that many of these seminar leaders are inadequately trained, indeed, often having become 'instant' practitioners of--and often 'instant' converts to--their craft without the clinical training and sophistication required to detect incipient breakdown and distress; and, further, that by their peregrination from city to city after but one or two sessions with their client groups in each, may leave in their wake many in confusion and turmoil through exposing latent emotional problems and aggravating unconscious fixations and complexes which, because of their abrupt departure from the encounter scene, cannot now

be ministered to by them, thus often leaving these now desperate clients without easy relief).

It is in this sense that the encounter group nurtures
anonymous or ritualized experience and sensation, however
differently they may appear to an observer or feel to those
undergoing them and however infrequently they occur in the
everyday world. Indeed, it is this infrequency that helps
give the impression that these experiences are deep, unusual,
and of rich significance. Also significant is their charade-
like quality--as if undergoing them were like being in a
dream or hypnagogic state or as if one were dissociated from
reality and were playing a role with only part of one's self
involved, and as if, though knowing this experience was illusory or make-believe--like a movie--yet taking it to be real.
In this sense, these encounter charades are often representations of silhouette selves--and so are analogous to the superficial charades and roles of business or of everyday interpersonal manipulation and maneuver. However, in the latter case, the fragmentation is of the shrewd, the acquisi-
tive, and the exploitative dimensions (or selves) from the
full human matrix of genuine affect, sensation, cognition and
realistic experience. So, too, is the encounter experience
often similarly fragmented except that in its case the functions that are extracted from the human matrix are exactly
those that are pushed aside in the everyday materialistic
world, i.e., the sensory, the affective, and the spiritual.

Consistent with the hyperdeveloped emphasis on separate
and dissociated sectors of behavior is the fact the pleasure
or excitement of encounter experiences is often one of their
salient goals: a feasting on them due possibly to their previous deprivation and a sort of childlike indulgence in their
most elementary forms which are devoid both of differentiated
development and of the cognitive components with which they
could be integrated. Rather like those of a child, these
experiences have a quality of self-indulgence, of excitement
for its own sake, of lack of concern with more extensive and
deeper issues and of unwillingness to confront certain aspects of external reality. In addition, because they do not
often occur in everyday life, they appear as titillating and
intriguing as children's new toys.

Indeed, the concern with feeling for itself without reference to purpose, direction, values enhanced, public policy
sustained, social organizations supported, way of life abetted, and image of man subserved is one of the characteristics
of this movement. Without question, it can be a healthy an-
tidote to the ritualization and ennui of the role-playing of
the day-to-day world except if these feelings, themselves,

become ritualized, the encounters, themselves, become affective role-playing games, and the procedures of inducing spontaneity and richer interpersonal relations become a product of a mechanistic mold. Beyond this, what must be remembered is that feeling qua feeling may lead to excesses of self-indulgence without reference to other values, human resources, or concern for others. This indulgence in feeling, by itself, without reference to human or social consequence may not, in principle, be different from the social psychologic matrix out of which emerge collective frenzies, hate manias, and other varieties of social or political fanaticisms. Such emotional indulgence can lead to vast collective delusions whether of persecutory, messianic, benign, or barbaric nature and to systematized escapist patterns and rituals. At the personal level, they may appear as impulse-ridden, excessively sensate, sensation-seeking, and yet other asymmetric forms of uninhibited affect.

It is here that the encounter movement reveals its affective promiscuity and valuative limbo--or possibly nihilism. For it is ready for all experience, all states of being, and all explorations of sensation. It is like Prospero's Ariel in The Tempest shouting, "Freedom, heigh day," but the question is what will become of Ariel when he grows up. It is like a desperately hungry man who will eat anything, a thirsty child who will drink brackish water as well as champagne not knowing how to judge them, or a sex-starved human who will sleep with any member of the opposite or the same sex.

Indeed, it is often the character of the encounter experience to stimulate sexual interest, intimacy, personal revelation, and the like without an enlightened basis being present for these interactions or without the emergence of a significant understanding essential to making them meaningful and constructive. Do not these types of contact often result in excitements without purpose or fulfillment: superficial sensations or titillations that are often mistaken for a significant and full-bodied experience but that, too frequently, are only provocations without genuine satisfaction?

Sometimes these encounters seem stripped of all but atomistic, unintegrated, and primitive instinctual or affective process as if all the humanistic issues of morality, values, social goals, and a philosophy of life had virtually little significance. It is as if the crucial factors were blocked instinctual, affective, or sensory impulses that should be liberated in these stereotyped encounter contacts and a hunger for elemental emotional fulfillment that could be speeded up, packaged (or ritualized), and almost instantly

gratified. How reminiscent this is of the other productive,
marketing, and advertising practices of our society that are
also directed to the ends of quick exploitation of economic
opportunities and quick profits.

In a certain sense, these hypertrophied and indiscriminate emotions are quite roughly what Spengler called "second
religiousness", i.e., exciting sensation and other intense
experience to drown the actual present-day temper of purposelessness and despair. In this sense, not only the motive of
the movement but also its nature is evangelical in character,
calling for the redemption and higher dedication of man
through the myth and themes of codified feeling, spirituality,
intimacy, mysticism, communion and collectivity, and ecstatic
religiousness.

But let us look at this affect in another light. The
emphasis on feeling, elementary sensory experience, interpersonal spontaneity, spiritual elevation, and esthetic delight is all understandable and valuable in the encounter
movement. These are precisely the qualities and themes
denied in the workaday world of mechanization, bureaucratization, and materialism. What is not so clear is the tena-
cious outcry against intellectualism, against historical
knowledge of the issues that the encounter movement wrestles
with, against putting "feeling" into a context of judgement
and reason, against a rational consideration of the emergent
forms and values of the emotional experiences that are
aroused in encounter sessions, against consideration of the
role and priorities that reason, morality, social goals, philosophy, and even expediency should have in the direction of
and relation with emotion, and against a detailed and balanced consideration of how feeling may contribute to human
wisdom and happiness and how it may not. Related, also, is
the resistance against the consideration of its optimal integration with a philosophy of life and salutary social ends,
its intelligent use to achieve thoughtfully or deeply valued
goals rather than to exclusively serve as a vehicle for pro-
miscuous expression, and its wise and proportionate outlay
with which to obtain optimal pleasure over a maximal interval
of time rather than its release in transitory, intensive, and
often jading indulgence.

It is in this sense that there exists a dissociation of
feeling from cognition and in this sense, too, that the encounter group movement can be said to be anti-intellectual.
For no question is consistently raised about the value of
such experience in yielding insight relative to the ends of a
salutary existence or to its role in the whole catalogue of
personal and collective human expression. Nor are the fur-

ther questions raised as to whether these experiences are
genuinely healthy, infantile, cathartic or unequivocally sensual, reflect a wish for an earlier childlike state, and the
like. Thus, affect, however paramount it is in the human
condition, is not examined--in the encounter movement--for
the authentic and vital functions it plays in actualized human life or for the goals it purports to subserve, nor
analyzed for the content and quality of its constituent pro-
perties, but rather is uncritically accepted as sufficient
unto itself. This is, in part, a child's view of affect and
may represent, too, a wish to return to a child's world.

But such a dissociation is mirrored in other aspects of
the encounter experience: the division between it's reju-
venating, warming, and releasing feelings on the one hand and
the callousing, dehumanizing, oppressive experiences of the
real world on the other. To be diverted from the latter,
affluent persons and especially those ridden with purposelessness or ennui are prepared to happily contribute for the
soothing balm of experiencing some spontaneous and humane
feelings and for the privilege of thinking of themselves as
genuinely human. Thereupon they can better sustain the
deadly and depersonalizing effects of the real world, indeed
often believing that the behavior they evince in it--manipu-
lative hard, opportunistic, callous--is not really so bad or
serious because their real selves, or substantial segments
of them, are so basically benign that their day-to-day acts
do not genuinely characterize their true nature. Indeed,
even when engaging in these acts, they do so--if they have
learned their lessons well in the encounter sessions--with a
smile and a graciousness and sensitivity that make them seem
more human to themselves, and possibly deceives others in the
same way. If this is true, what may be happening as a side
effect of these encounters is a vast escalation of guile,
double talk, double think, and circuses of sham and deception
calculated to hide and mitigate the impact of the harsh
everyday world that encounter group clients are convinced
will have no substantial deleterious effect on them--or they
on others--if they proficiently practice the encounter arts.
Is it possible that what issues from these experiences, then,
is a new trickiness, a new salesmanship, a new hypocrisy, or
a new set of contrived masks? Is it possible that the encounter group movement does not vitally evoke in its clients
the genuineness and courage to face the obstacles to humanism
in the real world and to resolve them with compassion, insight, and sensitivity? Rather it may be that it offers them
the illusion--or the ruse--that they are resolving these humanistic issues (particularly when they do so on week ends
and in seminars away from realistic confrontation with them)
or that they think they are now more courageously humanistic

than they were before they became encounter participants. Or do these sessions teach them the gambits and techniques of appearing to be humane, warm, and benevolent to others--as in the manner of good politicians and salesmen--while, in fact, disingenuously not precluding them from engaging in the same order and spirit of behavior as before, though now with a greater sense of diplomacy, sensitivity to interpersonal relations, and awareness of how to sweeten their hard purposes and actions and, indeed, of how to deceive others (and possibly also themselves) as to their genuine intent?

In effect, then, both crucibles of experience (the real world and the encounter world) are, in their separate ways, superficial and fragmented and agree in not acknowledging the total matrix of human experience including that of a broad philosophy of life, a full integration of feeling and intellect, or, in sum, a humanistic cognition. What the one emphasizes, the other de-emphasizes as if the stress on the shrewd, materialistic, and manipulative components of experience had to be compensated for by an equivalent stress on the affective, sensory, and spiritual components. Thus, in a wider context, both point to the main currents of dissociation of the times and to the lack of integration of basic and complementary sectors of experience with each other as well as into a fuller human matrix whether through hyperdevelopment or exclusion.

In such a broader canvas, the encounter movement can be seen as an expression of the disintegration of the coherence of a society, of the decline of its ruling spirit and ethos, and as the frenzied search for individual indulgence and pleasure inasmuch as its binding ties and organic value orientations have deteriorated. As a consequence, there is no longer a substantial human purpose, a cohesive value system, or a meaning that gives direction and significance to life and that provides a medium and goal in accord with which human beings can orient their work, the upbringing of their children, and the fabric of their lives. Because of this dissolution of the vital spirit and thrust of the society, humans are left without purpose, direction, personal meaning, and social or existential identity. As a consequence, personal alienation increases, authentic and meaningful personal relations are fragmented, the texture of group coherence and community commitment is undermined, and a sense of personal loneliness, abandonment, and isolation grows apace.

To these conditions, contemporary men--as did those in comparable stages of past historical cycles--react by an intensity of sensation-seeking, a thirst for excitement, and a drive for extremes of pleasure and violence. Such indul-

gences have the function of compensating for their spiritual
and existential death, for their social fragmentation, and
for their occupational mechanization. It is from such a
broad perspective that one must see the frantic urgency for
all sorts of thrills, for intense visual, auditory, or muscu-
lar stimulations, and for novelties of taste, whether they be
of interpersonal, physical, sensory, sexual, or other varieties. It is from despair and pessimism that such excitements
are bred in order to make men feel human and "alive" again.
Nor are these conditions unique to contemporary times. They
have occurred, historically, say Spengler (29) and Toynbee
(31), at each period when, like today, the ethos of society
has been fractured and man has lost his spiritual courage and
has suffered a failure of moral and human nerve. Thus, as
Roman power waned, such sensationalism grew rampant, marking
the impending decline of society as was the case in Byzantium
in the eleventh century and in Paris at the end of the ancien
régime.

From another view, the encounter group movement may represent an escape or diversion from the authentic humanistic
challenge of the day-to-day world by allowing its practitioners to get their humanistic fulfillments in those week ends
or seminars at which there is no serious threat to their
everyday mode of life, no immediate challenge to their daily
vested commitments or economic and materialistic interests,
and no serious jeopardy to their social positions in the established society of which they are a part. In this view the
sensory explorations, inner experience, and the like of the
encounter movement permit the luxury of humanistic-like indulgence, of liberated affect and sensation for an interval
of time and, possibly, of temporary renewal in order to return afterward to the depersonalization, interpersonal manipulation, and materialism of the "real" world that nurtured
the alienation and, as a result, the fragmented rebellion
against it. Thus, the division between the encounter group
movement and life reflects, in part, the very dissociation
between genuine interest and conformist activity, between
authentic humanistic experience and ritualized counterfeit
behavior, that the encounter group was designed to resolve.

In a sense, then, this form of encounter group orientation and its satellite experiences (sensory awakening, inner
meditation, affective excitement, and so on) is really a
middle-class recreation, a diversion, a relief from the
mechanization, dehumanization, and ennui that it was developed to confront and rectify. As such, the question must be
raised whether it is different from any other middle-class
recreation or diversion (in this connection, see the previously cited McCardel and Murray [20] paper)--a week end in

the country, a la dolce vita interlude, a trip to Europe, a
wild party, and the like--in its capacity for evoking authentic human feeling and experience. Is its function, then, in
these respects no more than that of affluent middle-class
"kicks" with a patina of sophisticated ideology and of avant-
garde, esoteric delight? Of course, it gives its participants a sense of being liberated, enlightened, and sophisticated in tune with the advanced themes of the day and the
movements of the young, and to that extent gives them a sense
of renewed youth and freshness--a brief diet of uninhibited-
ness that doubtless middle-class life sorely needs. But the
issue still remains whether this is any more than personal
release or indulgent recreation with a facade of sophisticated "advanced" ideology or myth to give it sanction and respectability.

For some, the world of encounter groups is not unlike
Viennese society between World War I and the coming of Hitler:
a society of hopelessness, desperation, and pretense. On
their comparable week ends, the Viennese middle class of the
day--affluent and directionless--would put on masks emulating
the various roles of the persons they would have liked to be:
lover, hero, pleasure-seeker, adventurer, explorer, and the
like--all the roles and functions in which they could not
participate in everyday life--and, like children in a make-
believe pantomine, would achieve the fantasied satisfaction
to sufficiently buoy them up to return with less ennui or as-
perity to their dreary everyday lives. Nor is the nature of
these week ends and seminar encounters, in the large historical view, substantially different from that of the pleasure-
seekers of Rome at the decline of the Empire, the court of
Charles II marking the end of the Restoration, the après moi
le déluge and fin-de-siècle excitements of the Bourbons before the Revolution. What did all these experiences amount
to: a last ecstatic and pleasurable gasp to hide the wounds
of despair and purposelessness; a frenzied excitement of sensation and thrills to mask the failure to confront the overwhelming issues of the real world--a world in which there
seemed no avenue for satisfaction of affirmative and vital
human impulse or in which the options for an authentic human
renewal and for purposeful and fulfilling resolution of the
deepest problems of human frustration, meaninglessness, and
corruption appeared unlikely to emerge.

Indeed, many of the middle-class persons who make up the
predominant constituency of encounter group participants (16)
and who are essential for the maintenance of established society are also those rather disenchanted with the psychologic
gratifications it offers them. Committed as they are through
tradition and training to the day-to-day roles they play, to

the status positions they enjoy, to the substantial incomes
they receive, and, in general, to the materialist gratifications and related establishment attitudes they acquire, it is
extremely difficult for them to directly confront worldly activities with genuine humanistic orientations or to analyze
them in terms of the humane and generous values they pursue
in the encounter experience, isolated as it is from the
authentically realistic world. For to do so might evoke
doubts about the means and ends of their income-pursuing
methods; raise skepticism about their support of or silence
on so many established institutions and status quo practices
that are antihumanistic, ritualized, and repressive of the
very values they say they wish to be realized; call into
question their day-to-day relationships with their colleagues,
business associates, or family; and, in general, raise dis-
concerting questions about their conformity, materialism,
acquisitiveness, overpracticality, cunning, repression of
free impulse, lack of interpersonal openness, and deficiency
of inner spiritual experience.

No wonder that these humanistic satisfactions, interpersonal delights, and sensory explorations are sought not in
the real world but rather out of it in the seminars, week
ends, and discussion groups where the hard, practical urgencies, status demands, and materialistic regards of authentic
day-to-day life are not operative. Here, one can indulge in
all these diverted and repressed delights without fear of
jeopardizing one's status, job, income, and, often enough,
related establishment attitudes. Thus, one may have one's
cake and eat it too. Indeed, the very dissociation between
these two worlds serves to sustain the viability of the practices followed in the real one while giving the impression,
by virtue of engaging in the diversionary encounter experiences, that one is genuinely humanistic or has dipped deeply
into the wellsprings of being a real human being. Thus,
while one feels humanistic, one is, at the same time, protected from applying this humanism too deeply, genuinely, or
perceptively to the institutions that subvert it.

Indeed, as already suggested, many aspects of encounter
group phenomena, represent what Spengler (29) called "second
religiousness" which he presumed to be the earmarks of societies in process of decay. In his view, the despair and
alienation accompanying such decay reveal themselves not only
in magnified and decadent displays of ritual and sensationalism but in more desperate and indiscriminate searches for
community, collectivity and love, as well.

"In a sense, the urgency for warmth, acceptance and
understanding that mark the encounter movement symbolizes

this search for community and inclusiveness, for such a
search is a reaction to the fragmentation and isolation of
contemporary life and a frantic effort to relive this condition by acquiring the personal qualifications and human techniques (warmth, spontaneity, sensitivity, etc.) necessary for
the development of and participation in such a humanistic
community. But in its desperate effort to remedy a condition
inherent in the nature of present society, this search often
takes diffuse and indiscriminate forms whether these be week
end encounter sessions or training in a sensitivity that it
is contended--possibly more in terms of utopian wishful thinking than in realistic assessment--will ensure the emergence
of community, if only an amorphous and play-fantasied one or
if only one confined to a few transient, undifferentiated or
charade-like relationships. By engaging in such encounter
activities, however much self-actualization, benevolence and
liberation of feelings they may provide, the mood of unthink-
ing desperation that originally gave rise to them--and that
may defensively conceal their more fundamental causes including those of vested economic, social and psychologic self-
interest and commitment--is revealed. For how else can we
explain that these practices take no account of the realities
of personal interest and temperament, or of the social and
economic nature of the everyday world in which such a community must be established, or of the authentic humanistic
components (including cognition and values) that are often
more honored by neglect than by observance. What does seem
to passionately matter is the urgency to satisfy the desire
for human fellowship and community; indeed, it is from this
passionate desperation that comes the unwillingness to ask
the central and courageous question as to how such a humanistic community can be established in the real world which is
its worst enemy and, indeed, the root cause for its frantic
search. When this question has been carefully posed and
answered, a substantial advance will have been made in the
conception of the humanistic community, and the schism between its search in the encounter group and in the real world
will have been more closely bridged" (27, pp. 465-66).

If the lack of examination of these and other crucial
human conditions and values is a result of a lack of social
or historical awareness and a general anti-intellectualism
stemming from an absence of genuine direction or philosophy,
the encounter group movement may be afflicted with the same
meaninglessness and purposelessness it was designed to remedy
and with a comparable dissociation from vital reality, authentic earthy feeling, and deep human interest that it was generated to counteract. If this is true, it would be as atomistic, meaningless, and counterfeit--though in the realms of
emotion, spirituality and sensation--as the mechanized, ritu-

alized life it presumes to confront.

Further, if the cause of this dissociation is, indeed, a lack of valuative direction, then it is not clear which image of man or philosophy of life these liberated feelings and sensations should be directed to subserve. Surely there are as many humanistic images of man (26) and as many diverse philosophies of life as there are sensations and affects to explore, as many types of self-actualization as there are human resources, and as many social organizations and ideal societies as there are varieties of interpersonal relations.

But here the encounter movement leaves us in limbo, as full of puzzled doubt and uncertainty as it claims is the condition of contemporary man in his struggles with the modern mechanized world. For surely with each different image of man, philosophy of life, or system of values, quite different types of sensation, feeling and interpersonal experience would ensue.[1] For example, if justice were conceived to be an all-consuming end of life as well as a directing philosophy of the encounter movement, there possibly would be less tendency to encourage certain types of interpersonal behavior and more to encourage and explore others; viz., there might be a less tolerant view of personal excitements and pleasures--particularly at the expense of others-- and possibly more concern with experiences that fuse others in sympathy and compassion or with those that generate attitudes of fair and just treatment of them. To apply such specific humanistic values or goals to the encounter movement itself, there would be, for example, more concern with the scale of fees charged for seminars and group meetings, more concern for soliciting lower-class and minority-group clients, more awareness and possibly dismay about the profit motive of various of the growth centers, and more concern, too, with the economic motives and self-aggrandizement of various of the seminar leaders.

For these and other reasons and because all perception and response are related to an implicit or explicit value context or system of societal norms, there can be, it appears, no way of eliminating moral, social, and collective issues from the very conception and onset of the encounter group experience. Otherwise, anarchy, unreflected bias, and a blooming, buzzing confusion of experience would result. Thus, though there must be no discounting of the great salutary im-

---

[1]The nature of the relationship between these various factors have been richly explored both in historical and contemporary times in The Images of Man by Bernard G. Rosenthal, (Basic Books, 1971).

portance of the liberation of affect and sensation and the
opening to new experience that the encounter group provides,
this must be placed simultaneously in context with issues
such as: To what end is it directed?   For what group?   To
what image or vision of man does it speak?   For what society
will it be beneficial?

These issues must be faced wisely and courageously, and
questions must be asked such as: What is the nature of the
morality involved in superficial and transient emotional relationships precipitously induced for a short interlude?
What type of emotional training is being given in encounter
groups for a bureaucratic, mechanized society where sensory
and affective openness and humanistic values ought to be
brought into every sector of life in a way that takes full
account of the complexities and obstacles that the present
cultural system, with its materialistic preoccupations and
intense competitions, presents to their full realization and
whose socio-economic structure, therefore, may have to be
modified or transformed before the humanistic ethos can be
genuinely implemented?   Only when the question is squarely
raised as to whether those practices and experiences enable
men to be more humanistic, generous, and liberated in their
everyday existence, only when the ends of awareness, sensitivity, compassion, appreciation of beauty, and the like are
related to the life of the real world and to our present social system can the experiences of the encounter group and
its allied activities be put fully into balance and assessed.

REFERENCES

1. Bach, G. R. "Marathon Group Dynamics: II. Dimensions of Helpfulness: Therapeutic Aggression." Psychol. Reports, 1967, 20, 1147-1158.

2. Bach, G. R. "Discussion." Int. J. Group Psychother., 1968, 18, 244-249.

3. Bebout, J., and Gordon, B. "The Value of Encounter." Paper presented at AAAS Section on Psychological Sciences--Encounter Groups, 1971, Philadelphia.

4. Cadden, J. J. et al. "Growth in Medical Students Through Group Process." Amer. J. Psychiatry, 1969, 126, 862-867.

5. Campbell, J. P., and Dunnette, M. D. "Effectiveness of T-Group Experiences of Managerial Training and Development." Psychol. Bull., 1968, 70, 73-104.

6. Crawshaw, R. "How Sensitive is Sensitivity Training?" Amer. J. Psychiat., 1969, 126, 868-74.

7. Freeland, R. C. "Some Effects of Verbal Feedback on Perceptions of Members in Two Marathon Encounter Groups." Ed.D. thesis. Diss. Abst. Int. 1973. Univ. M-Films, No. 73-25510, 197 pp.

8. Geddes, P. Cities in Evolution. London: Williams and Worgate, 1915.

9. Gottschalk, L. A. "Psychoanalytic Notes on T-Groups at the Human Relations Laboratory, Bethel, Maine." Comprehensive Psychiatry, 1966, 7, 472-487.

10. Gottschalk, L. A., and Pattison, E. M. "Psychiatric Perspectives on T-Groups and the Laboratory Movement: An Overview." Amer. J. Psychiat., 1969, 126, 823-40.

11. Kasserjian, H. H. "Social Character and Sensitivity Training." J. Applied Behav. Sci., 1965, 1, 433-40.

12. Kernan, J. P. "Laboratory Human Relations Training: Its Effects on the 'Personality' of Supervisory Engineers." Dissertation Abstracts, 1964, 25, 665-66.

13. Kuehn, J. L., and Crinella, F. M. "Sensitivity Training: Interpersonal Overkill and Other Problems." Amer. J. Psychiat., 1969, 126, 841-46.

14. Lazarus, A. A. Behavior Therapy and Beyond. New York: McGraw-Hill, 1970.

15. Lieberman, M. A. "Change Induction in Small Groups." Annual Review of Psychology, 1976, 27, 217-250.

16. Lieberman, M. A. and Gardner, J. "Institutional Alternatives to Psychotherapy; A Study of Growth Center Users." Arch. Gen. Psychiatry, 1976, 33, 157-162.

17. Lieberman, M. A., Yalom, I. D., and Miles, M. B. "Encounter Groups: Their Effects and Sources of Effects." Paper presented at AAAS Section on Psychological Sciences--Encounter Groups, 1971, Philadelphia.

18. Lieberman, M. A., Yalom, I. D., and Miles, M. B. Encounter Groups: First Facts. New York; Basic Books, 1973.

19. Lima, F. P., and Lievano, J. E. "Personal Communication." 1968, (in Parloff, M. B. Int. J. Group Psychother., 1970, 20, (1), 14-24.)

20. McCardel, J. and Murray, E. J. "Non-specific Factors in Weekend Encounter Groups". J. Consult. Clin. Psychol., 1974, 42, 337-45.

21. McLeish, J. and Park, J. "Outcomes Associated with Direct and Vicarious Experience in Training Groups: II. Attitudes, Dogmatism." Brit. J. Soc. Clin. Psychol., 1973, 12, 353-58.

22. Miles, M. B. "Changes During and Following Laboratory Training: A Clinical-Experimental Study." J. Applied Behav. Sci., 1965, 1, 215-242.

23. Mintz, E. C. "Marathon Groups: A Preliminary Evaluation." J. Contemporary Psychother., 1969, 1, 91-94.

24. Parloff, M. B. "Group Therapy and the Small Group Field: An Encounter." Int. J. Group Psychother., 1970, 20 (1) 14-24.

25. Rogers, C. R. "The Process of the Basic Encounter Group." in Bugental, J.F.G. (Ed.): Challenges of Humanistic Psychology, New York: McGraw-Hill, 1967.

26. Rosenthal, B. G. The Images of Man. New York: Basic Books, 1971.

27. Rosenthal, B. G. "The Nature and the Development of the Encounter Group Movement.: in Confrontation: Encounters in Self and Interpersonal Awareness. (Ed. L. Blank & G. Gottsegen) 435-468. New York: The MacMillan Co., 1971.

28. Rosenthal, B. G. "Encounter Groups: Facts, Explanations, and Values." Paper presented at AAAS Section on Psychological Sciences--Encounter Groups, 1971, Philadelphia.

29. Spengler, O. The Decline of the West. New York: Alfred A. Knopf, 1926.

30. Taylor, F. C. "Effects of Laboratory Training upon Persons and Their Work Groups." in Zalkind, S. S. (Chairman), Research on the Impact of Using Different Laboratory Methods for Interpersonal and Organizational Change. (Symposium presented at the Meeting of the American Psychological Association, Washington, D. C., September 1967.)

31. Toynbee, A. A Study of History. Abridgement of Vol. I-X by D. C. Somervell. New York: Oxford University Press, 1947-57.

32. Yalom, I. D., and Lieberman, M. A. "A Study of Encounter Group Casualties." Archives of General Psychiatry, 1971, 25, 16-30.

33. Yalom, I. D. et al. "Encounter Groups and Psychiatry." Task Force Report No. 1. Washington, D. C., American Psychiatric Association, 1970.

Benjamin D. Zablocki is associate professor of sociology at Columbia University, concentrating in urban sociology and sociology of the family. He is the author of The Joyful Community *(Penguin, 1971).*

5

Communes, Encounter Groups and the Search for Community

Benjamin D. Zablocki

Let us start with an assumption that is rea-
sonably self-evident: encounter group attenders
and commune members are seekers for new life-
styles. Both the encounter group movement and the
contemporary communitarian movement originated in
the United States in the mid-1960's and flourished
in the decade 1965-1975. This decade also saw a
proliferation of diverse life-styles.

The coterminous duration of communitarian and
encounter group movements and their common association with the collective search for new styles of
identity leads one to ask in what way these two
movements are related. Are they both expressions
of cultural and demographic needs peculiar to the
decade in question? Are they best understood as
specific aspects of some larger and more encompassing social movement? Did they develop independently of one another or are there mutual or one-
way causal influences which can be discovered?
This paper will be devoted to a discussion of some
evidence bearing on each of these questions in
turn.

Cultural and Demographic Origins

The emergence of the counterculture and life-
style experimentation has taken place among people
for whom occupational and economic role no longer
provided a coherent set of values and for whom
identity has come to be generated in the consumption rather than the production realm, and affluence has permitted a choice of goods from which to
make up a life-style package. For Bell (1), indeed, one sign of the coming of the post-industrial

society was the relative independence of the production, consumption, and distribution realms: that for many participants, each system operated by different principles and different rules. Individuals are relatively free to make a range of independent, even hedonistic, consumption decisions little constrained by their productive roles. Therefore it is perilous to make the assumption that either all encounter group attenders or all commune members are part of a monolithic social movement. Nevertheless, to simplify discussion, motivational distinctions within these rubrics will not be discussed until the third part of this paper.

It is important to distinguish life-style from stage in the life cycle. When SES is held constant the best remaining predictor of life-style, as measured by consumer behavior, is stage in life cycle (2). There has been a tendency, therefore, to over-identify particular life-styles with their modal age cohorts, ignoring the wide range in age distribution actually found among the adherents of most life-styles. Thus, for example, communes have been treated as a youth phenomenon, although there is evidence that about a quarter of all members of contemporary American communes are over the age of thirty (3). Such age-cohort stereotyping of life-styles could conceivably blind researchers to the role of broadly based life-styles in transforming culture.

Nevertheless, many of the adherents of alternative life-styles are undoubtedly recruited from a certain few life stages whose developmental tasks require experimentation (4). The amorphous period between adolescence and adulthood that has been identified as youth (5) involves a great deal of life-style experimentation. So does the equally amorphous period following the increasingly common event—termination of first marriage (6). Less extensively, and for somewhat different reasons, the final period of life, after retirement from work and child-rearing, tends to be associated with life-style experimentation (7). Let us examine how each of these age-groups fared, demographically and culturally, during the period 1965-1975.

Youth

During the period 1965 to 1975, a glut of youth appeared within American society. Two causes

of a glut are over-adequacy of supply and inadequacy of demand. During the period we are discussing, the over-adequacy of supply resulted from the
baby boom of 1945-1960. The causes of inadequacy
of demand are more complex. They have to do primarily with changes in the nature and composition
of the American labor force. As Figure One shows,
the proportion of youth (population aged fifteen to
twenty-four) to the older adult population (aged
twenty-five to sixty-four) bulged during the period
1965 to about 1975.*

In an analysis of the demographic characteristics of American youth, Havighurst argues that this
phenomenon of glut is clearly delimited in time and
that we should therefore be seeing a recovery of
the institutions of socialization after 1975:

> Every society must ingest a generation
> of children and digest or socialize them
> into adults who can carry on the business
> of the society. The process sometimes
> gives the society discomfort, and that
> is happening in the 1970's to the Ameri-
> can society...
>
> If our assumptions hold, the presently
> growing numbers of youth ready to enter
> the labor force will stabilize after 1975,
> and the society will then absorb youth
> more easily than it has been able to do
> during the period from 1965 to 1975.(8)

Although there may be reason to doubt whether
the process of recovery for the institutions of socialization will be as smooth as this, nevertheless
there is evidence that the cohorts of young people
born after 1960 are sharply different in attitude,
especially in attitudes toward counterculture movements and towards the legitimacy of societal institutions than were the individuals born in the fifteen years prior to that. During more demographi-

---

*This proportion, however, is not extraordinar-
ily high in comparison to the early part of this
century (primarily for reasons of increased life
expectancy and a very high birth rate during the
early part of the century), though it is quite a
bit higher than the period both before and after.

FIGURE 1

RATIO OF POPULATION AGED 15 - 24
TO POPULATION AGED 25 - 64
1900 - 2000

Table taken from Youth; The Seventy-fourth
Yearbook of the National Society for the Study of
Education, R. J. Havighurst and P. Dreyer, Eds.
University of Chicago Press, Chicago, 1975), p. 127.

cally normal times, the cohorts of young people between the ages of fifteen and twenty-five would be
absorbed into society largely through participation
in the labor force, through marriage and early family formation, and through the process of higher
education.

Post-Protogamy

In the absence of any existing term to denote
first marriage, let us coin the term, "protogamy."
The open-ended period following the termination of
first marriage (whether or not there is ever to be
a second marriage) we may then call the post-protogamous phase of the life cycle. Irreverent as
the phrase may sound, this phase has come to be a
reality for increasing numbers of people. It is
crucial for our purposes because the most committed, if not the most numerous, segments of the mem-
berships of both encounter groups and communes are
recruited from the post-protogamous.

In the period from 1965 to 1975, the moral
value structure of American society changed radically to the point where a wide variety of living
situations for young couples other than marriage
became acceptable. This, along with a tendency for
women to enter into serious educational and career
roles, has led to a drastic reduction in the number
of people in the 20 to 25 year age range who married. Meanwhile the percentages of males and females who are separated or divorced has increased
significantly. (See Figure Two.) Although the
comparable figures for the 25 to 30 year old cohort
indicate that a certain amount of this marriage de-
crease is simply marriage delay, there may be more
to the picture than that. According to Glick (9):

> ...it is too early to predict with confi-
> dence that the increase in singleness
> among the young will lead to an eventual
> decline in life-time marriage [but],
> just as cohorts of young women who have
> postponed childbearing for an unusually
> long time seldom make up for the child
> deficit as they grow older, so also
> young people who are delaying marriage
> may never make up for the marriage defi-
> cit later on. They may try alternatives
> to marriage and they may like them.

FIGURE 2

TRENDS IN AMERICAN MARRIAGE

Trends in Marital Status 1970-1975[a]

Year	Married	Divorced	Separated	Single	Widowed
MEN					
1975	62.3	3.3	1.6	29.5	2.4
1970	64.3	2.2	1.3	28.1	2.9
% Change 1970 to 1975:	-3.1	+50.0	+23.0	+4.9	-17.2
WOMEN					
1975	56.9	4.8	2.8	22.8	12.1
1970	58.4	3.5	2.2	22.1	12.5
% Change 1970 to 1975	-2.6	+37.1	+27.2	+3.1	-3.2

[a]Percentage of total U.S. population 14 years of age and over.

Source: Jessie Bernard, "Note on Changing Life Styles, 1970-1974," Journal of Marriage and the Family 37 (1975), p. 583. Also U.S. Bureau of the Census, Current Population Reports, P-20, no. 287, "Marital Status and Living Arrangements: March 1975." (Washington, D.C.: U.S. Government Printing Office, 1975), Table 1.

Peter Stein, Singles, (Harper and Row, New York, 1976).

Since most people do marry at least once, and since the great majority of young people continue to re-port the strong intention of marrying (at least once), intentional spinsterhood or bachelorhood probably do not merit serious consideration as emerging life-styles. Absorption into the post-protogamous state, albeit often for short periods

of time, is a more significant destabilizing event.
To the extent that marriage in the past served as a
stabilizing factor and socialized individuals into
adult roles, we can see that this means that there
are larger proportions of people who are not subject to these influences in 1975 than there were in
1965. The large-scale postponement of the bearing
of the first child on the part of large numbers of
families for those that do marry also results in
larger numbers of individuals free for life-style
experiments.

One other aspect of the family problem should
be discussed in this section, and that is the long-
term secular trend of isolation of the nuclear family from extended family network affiliations.
This trend has been clouded somewhat by the excellent works of historical demography by Laslett, et
al., (10) dispelling certain myths about the preva-
lence of three-generational families in the past.
Unfortunately, this welcome dispelling of the romantic myth of the three-generational family has
led to an overreaction. The social scientists 20
or 30 years ago saw the distinction in absolute
terms. Urban industrial nuclearization of the family was contrasted to a romantic image of the pre-
industrial extended family. Corrections of this
view should not obscure the fact that a less dramatic trend towards isolation of the nuclear family
has undoubtedly occurred. We will return to this
problem in discussing old age.

The institution of marriage and family has a
dual impact on the social movements under investi-
gation: on the one hand, delayed and terminated
marriage and childbearing free a large proportion
of young people for low risk life-style experimentation; on the other hand, a breakup of extended
network ties of nuclear families may lead to total
kinship isolation as a consequence of widowhood,
separation, or divorce. This has led to the attempt to reconstitute less restrictive extended familial bonds based upon friendship or ideology,
rather than on marital and blood relationships.
These may be sought ephemerally in encounter groups
or, with somewhat more continuity, in communes.

Old Age

The problem of nuclear family isolation has consequences not only for the post-protogamous but for the old as well. The decade 1965-1975 saw a relative increase in the numbers of elderly in the population. The isolation of nuclear families through geographical mobility over the past several decades has served to doom many of the elderly to residence in one-person households.

The proportion of households occupied by only one person has been increasing, not only in big cities, but nationwide. Johnson and Herron (11) report the following:

> More and more of New York City's 8 mil-
> lion residents, by choice or for reasons
> they cannot control, are living alone.
> A study by the Community Council of
> Greater New York shows that a quarter of
> the city's households in 1970 were occu-
> pied by one person, compared with only a
> fifth in 1960.

> The trend results from a tendency among
> young people to set up households sepa-
> rate from their families, the fact that
> elderly people increasingly live alone
> rather than move in with their children
> and the frequency of divorce and return
> for many to the "singles" existence.

> The city has traditionally attracted
> young unattached and "upwardly mobile"
> people who can afford to live by them-
> selves. But the elderly poor make up a
> sizable proportion of those now living
> alone.

> In 1970, the study said, more than a
> third of the people by themselves were 65
> or over, an increase of 72 per cent over
> a decade. (12)

Belcher analyzed the demographic trend toward one-person household residence in this way:

> The one-person households are increas-
> ing more rapidly than the general popula-

tion. It may be noted that this increase
cannot be attributed simply to the changing age characteristics of the population.

In general, the incidence of people living alone increases with age. The relationship between age and living arrangements is so direct that it is suggested
that there is a living arrangement cycle
that is probably of great significance to
understanding our society. Such a cycle
is believed to provide some insight into
the creation and eventual dissolution of
the one-person household....

the data do permit the inference that
those living alone do exist largely outside the family system, be it nuclear or
extended. The entire analysis has shown
that those people who would appear to have
no or few living relatives are much more
prone to live alone than those who are
more likely to have surviving relatives
living near them.(13)

Old people have turned to communal living and
to encounter to cope with the problems of social
isolation although less frequently than have the
young and the post-protogamous. Old people attempting to live communally may face obstacles not
encountered by the young. In Florida, one commune
of the elderly had to fight a court battle to avoid
eviction from their home in a neighborhood that was
"not zoned for nursing homes."

Twelve active oldsters, who formed a
commune in a 27-room mansion to save
money, love each other as a "family" and
may continue to live together despite a
single-unit zoning law, a judge has
ruled....

After a 40-minute visit Thursday with
the elderly occupants and the 10-member
family which keeps the home in working
order, Judge Edwards said: "I have found
these people are not in violation of the
zoning ordinance.

"The whole atmosphere is very homelike
and warm, everyone seems to genuinely
care about each other, it is personalized
and spotlessly clean and really a delightful
place where everyone seems to be extremely
happy(14)."

However, Hochschild(15) has reported
that frequent deaths among peers may have a
demoralizing effect on attempts by the elderly to
stave off isolation by encountering or communing
together.

Cultural Elusiveness of Community

Communes and encounter groups were only the
most dramatic aspects of a generally heightened
concern with community as a dimension of lifestyle
during the period 1965-1975(16). Certain
enterprising housing developers responded to
this heightened concern by featuring community
themes in their building developments. In
California, one developer advertised a new type of
residence arrangement for young singles which he
called the "communium" (cross between commune and
condominium), and which featured a greater degree
of collectivization, especially in kitchen and
dining facilities, than had hitherto been available
in the American rented housing market. In
Tennessee, another clever builder reported that he
had saved a considerable amount of money by
developing his latest urban housing complex for
upper middle class young marrieds around an
organic farm rather than the usual golf course.
In a newspaper interview, he pointed out that such
a farm held greater cultural appeal for many of
his prospective home buyers than would a golf
course, was no more expensive to build, and was
considerably cheaper to maintain than a golf
course. It also provided the additional benefits
of cheap, fresh vegetables and optional therapeutic
manual labor for the young executive commuters for
whom the project was designed. Yet, for all these
efforts, genuine community has proven an elusive
experience.

Bennett Berger (17) has argued that
"the most durable and effective subcultures in the
United States have been the ones which combine

class, ethnic, and religious factors to create a
symbolically closed community." He contrasts the
full cultural life that is experienced, for example
in the Jewish ghetto and to a greater extent in the
Amish rural communities, with open cultural
identifications of the great majority of Americans,
whether urban or suburban in location. Suttles(18)
has demonstrated convincingly that the quest
for community, has characterized many of the
important social movements of the past decade in
fact reflects a desire for the cultural integrity
that is attributed to such closed, isolated
enclaves. He argues the following:

> A. . . likely consequence of the quest
> for community of sentiment--one where
> everyone can be his true moral self--is
> that the utopian images evoked tend to
> make insignificant any actual communities
> that have existed. . . . Such utopias
> are a powerful lure tempting us to
> reconstruct history and dismiss the present.

James Coleman (19) has suggested that we
may currently be experiencing a transformation
from geographical to non-geographical bases for
community in advanced societies. A number of
writers have discussed the professions, labor
unions, interest groups, and even encounter groups
as examples of such communities. Religious cults,
sects, and denominations, racial and ethnic groups,
and extended kinship networks have served this
function in the past and some continue to do so
today. Nevertheless, the overwhelming majority of
people still experience community primarily on the
residential level. Even when it occurs
spontaneously, community requires an infra-
structure to keep it going. It is not merely an
epiphenomenon. A profession or voluntary
association must nourish this infra-structure out
of a surplus of its members' invested resources, if
any such surplus remains after the manifest goals
of the group are met. The great advantage of the
residential community over other types is that, in
the residential community, proximity itself
provides for the greater part of the maintenance of
this infra-structure without the deliberate
intention of the individuals involved. Gerald
Suttles (20) has provided a good explanation of
how this comes about:

Copresence alone makes people captive
judges of each other's conduct and
requires them to develop at least some
communicative devices for anticipating
and interpreting each other's judgments
. . . . The enduring character of
territorial membership and the lack of
alternatives keeps groups together
willfully or unwillfully and makes short-
run opportunism a dangerous proposition,
since the opportunist must continue to
live with his victims. Similarly, the
involuntary confinement of such a group
allows its members to gain an intimate
knowledge of each other's personal
character, abilities at joint and artful
tasks, and the highly specialized routines
which any cooperative group must develop
on its own. Territoriality then, builds
accountability into a society without
anyone's having to work at it. . . . One
of the difficulties faced by some other
groupings, such as social classes,
intellectual circles, or interest groups,
is that their members can easily shift
sides, avoid one another, or engage in
transient relations. Such groupings may
not survive, because their members can
be fickle.

However, the cultural basis of residential
community has been eroding for quite some time in
American society under the forces of geographical
and social mobility. In the 1960's, the civil
rights movements helped to destroy such devices as
restrictive covenants and exclusionary zoning
whereby the poor and the colored were denied access
to many residential areas. Although this was
beneficial to the society it was harmful to
community. The free-rider effect, familiar to
political economists, discourages investment of time
and resources in any collectivity which cannot
restrict its membership.

Manifestations of a Larger Social Movement

Where community arises naturally out of the
mere fact of proximity or as the result of events
not deliberately aimed at the creation of a
community, let us use the term spontaneous

community. I will argue that communes and
encounter groups represent responses to the waning
of spontaneous community, and that they have a
particular role to play in the gradual replacement
of spontaneous residential communities by organized
residential communities within American society.
In particular, I will argue that the communes and
encounter groups may be thought of as experiments
in which elements of family, religion, and
neighborhood are blended in hitherto unknown (and
sometimes bizarre) ways, only a small fraction of
which prove viable.

If my argument is correct, then contemporary
American communes, unlike the Israeli kibbutzim or
the American utopian communities of the nineteenth
century, are not to be evaluated with respect to
their successes in the economic and political
spheres (aside from the minimal successes of
economic and political survival), but rather with
respect to their successes with what I shall call,
collectively, the institutions of identity.

FIGURE 3

Institutions of Identity (Being)	Institutions of Interest (Doing)
Religion	Economics
Family	Political
Neighborhood	Military

←——————— Education ———————→

To make such a distinction between the institutions
of identity and the institutions of interest is
to postulate that there exists, either in fact or
in popular definition, a distinction between
matters of action and matters of essence, a
philosophic question that has by no means been
resolved. This distinction is helpful, however, in
explaining a number of distinguishing facts about
encounter groups and communes:

     ---   low degree of investment in economic
           and political activities and in

        territorial defense within the
        group;

---   high degree of investment in familial,
        religious, and cooperative activities
        within the group;

---   attempt at thoroughgoing disaffiliation
        from the economic, political, and
        military activities of the larger
        community on the part of many communes;

---   continued affiliation (unlike the
        nineteenth century utopias) with
        families of origin, with religious
        groups in the larger society, and
        with non-group neighbors i.e.,
        anti-exclusivity);

---   a tendency for collective innovations
        to be concerned with familial,
        religious, and neighborly relationships
        and, moreover, to involve the creation
        of role definitions and organizations
        of activity without respect to the
        demarcations by which the larger
        society ordinarily distinguishes these
        three institutions.

Let us then turn to an examination of communes and
encounter groups in terms of each of the
institutions of identity.

        Needleman (21)   has discussed the
appearance and rapid growth of religious sects
devoted to oriental religions in America. Zen
Buddhism from Japan; a variety of theological and
Yogic religious ideas from India; Subud from
Indonesia; and Sufism from the Middle East have all
gained a fair number of adherents and established
stable, ongoing religious organizations in America
within the past fifteen years. All of these
movements have in common the attempt to transcend
material concerns and gain an awareness of the
cosmic unity of all life and experience. This is
seen particularly clearly in some of the newer
of these movements--the Divine Light Movement and
the Movement for Krishna Consciousness, both of
which promote a totally introspective evaluation of
self-knowledge and an abandonment of attachment to

material things. Lofland (22) offers a picture
of the characteristics of seekers and process of
conversion in one such sect. Veysey (23) sees
such groups as outgrowths of recurrent mystical
themes in American cultural radicalism.

Similar etherealization has been exemplified
in the growth of the encounter-group movement and
related movements stressing value of relating and
turning on. Gustaitis (24), Leonard (25),
and Smith (26) have provided discussions of the
development of these lifestyles. Although
lifestyles characterized by spiritual etherealization remain for the most part anti-intellectual,
there has been in the last few years a tendency to
blend aspects of the spiritual and of the emotional
within the same lifestyle.

The evolving relationship of the American Jews
to a larger American society and culture
illustrates how new lifestyles can be built out of
the materials of old subcultures. Goren (27)
provides an excellent historical ethnographic
account of the original attempts to set up a
Kehillah (a totally encompassing apparatus for
community responsibility and control among the New
York Jews during the early part of the twentieth
century along the model of similar communal
organizations that had existed in Europe). Such a
Kehillah might have provided an enduring basis for
American Jewish value coherence. However, the
incompatibility of American pluralism with the
existence of closed communal enclaves of any size
and importance in an urban setting led to the
abandonment of this idea and to its replacement by
what Sklare (28) has referred to as the
subcommunity. Regarding the idea of a
subcommunity, Sklare states:

If American social organization did
not encourage groups who wish to
establish themselves as fullfledged
communities and if European models were
considered neither achievable nor
desirable by American Jews, American
society did offer an alternative: the
subcommunity. The subcommunity is a
community of sentiment rather than of
coercion. It exists within the inter-
stices of the social order and accommodates

itself to that order. The subcommunity
is a community of association. Such
associationalism can be strong; a
subcommunity may be the prime focus of
the individual's social attachments.
Nevertheless, it is not accorded an
official standing; the rights of the
individual are derived from the status
as a citizen rather than from the status
as a member of a group. Furthermore,
loyalty to the subcommunity is presumed
consistent with loyalty to the community
and the remote situation in which loyalty
to community and subcommunity conflict,
society expects that the subcommunity
will modify its program, defer its
demands, and demonstrate its loyalty to
the concept that the needs of the
community have primacy.

In recent years, however, the Jewish
subcommunity has foundered on the issue of value
incoherence. Significant numbers of individuals
desire for there to be a greater degree of value
coherence than comes about naturally through the
participation in a subcommunity of voluntary
association. In response to this in the late
1960's a proliferation of more tightly knit and
value-constraining Jewish fellowship organizations
known as Havarim (29) occurred in cities and
suburbs. These fellowships provided strong
network support for the stylistic revival of many
of the external identifiers of the Jewish
ethnicity.

Figure Four illustrates a similar pattern
with respect to Christian Churches. With
hardly an exception, those churches stressing
encounter and communion have grown significantly
faster than those stressing ethics and theology.
Even within the Catholic Church (generally the
most immune to historical social movements)
the development and growth of the Charismatic
Movement bears eloquent testimony to the
pervasive power of the encountering need in
religious life in the past decade.

FIGURE 4

Rank Order of Percentage of Membership Gains
for 16 Religious Bodies, 1940-1970 and
Percentage Increase in U.S. Population

Denominations	% Gain 1970 over 1940
1. Church of God (Cleveland)	332
2. Assemblies of God	224
3. Church of Jesus Christ of Latter-day Saints	186
4. Seventh-day Adventists	139
5. Southern Baptist Convention	136
6. Christian Reformed Church	134
7. Church of the Nazarene	131
8. Roman Catholic Church	127
9. Lutheran Church-Missouri Synod	118
10. Church of God (Anderson)	103
11. Presbyterian Church in the U.S.	80
12. The Episcopal Church	65
POPULATION OF THE UNITED STATES	58
13. United Presbyterian Church in the U.S.	43
14. United Methodist Church	33
15. United Church of Christ	15
16. American Baptist Convention	-5

(11-16 bracketed as: National Council of Churches (NCC))

Even allowing for some error in reporting
statistics or some technical factors not reported,
a direct correlation develops related to degree of
conservatism and strictness and high growth in
membership. At the top of the list we see the
Pentecostal bodies and other conservative groups
and at the bottom the NCC-related "liberal"
communions occupying places 11-16, with four of the
six bodies growing at a slower pace than the rate
of population increase for the Nation. Four of
the six NCC-related bodies recorded a lower membership in 1970 than in 1960, and five of six showed
declines of membership when one compares 1971
membership totals with those reported for 1970(30).

Encounter group and commune movements often seek to blend elements of religion and elements of family life in a manner which is foreign to our own culture, but quite the norm in cross-cultural perspective. Communes, and to some extent even encounter groups, may be viewed as attempts to find new forms for family life. Thousands of little groups experimenting with new forms for the family are interesting for at least two reasons. First, they suggest a certain amount of serious discontent with the traditional form of the family. Second, they provoke curiosity as to whether any of the experiments will succeed. Recently communes have been called "alternatives" to the traditional family system, both by a number of academic commentators and, increasingly, by spokesmen for the communes themselves. Thus far, however, no communitarian form has proven itself either popular enough or viable enough to be classified as a true alternative. Nevertheless, enough evidence exists, both of the decline of the traditional nuclear family and of the short-term viability of some of the communitarian forms, to justify continued interest.

By traditional nuclear family, I mean a collectivity composed of one husband, one wife, and a number of their children. This collectivity lives together for an extended period of time in its own separate dwelling unit. There is a full-time housekeeper (usually either the wife or an employee). In the traditional form, too, there is a considerable variance in the number of children per family.

In terms of Figure Five, a society in which the traditional nuclear family predominates takes on the following values:

Nuclear completeness (husband, wife, children)	high
Neolocality	high
Residential mobility	low
Housekeeping as a full-time profession	high

FIGURE 5

Indicators of the Decline of the Traditional
Nuclear Family Household in the Post-War Period

Variable and Indicator (for references, see notes)	Measurement (in %) Earliest	Latest
NUCLEAR COMPLETENESS:		
children in single-parent families	14% (1960)	23% (1970)
married couples (with husband under 35 years old) with no children living at home	18.4 (1960)	25 (1972)
households with male heads	85 (1950)	80 (1967)
NEOLOCALITY:		
married couples without own households	9 (1947)	1.5 (1968)
RESIDENTIAL MOBILITY:		
Residential telephones disconnected per year	17 (1946)	25 (1971)
HOUSEKEEPING AS A FULL-TIME PROFESSION: working age women in the labor force:		
all women	33.9 (1950)	43.8 (1972)
married women with husbands present	23.8 (1950)	41.5 (1972)
mothers of pre-school children	12 (1950)	30 (1972)
professional housekeepers in the labor force (in millions, not %)	2.5 (1960)	1.6 (1970)

Figure 5, continued

Variable and Indicator (for references, see notes)	Measurement (in %)	
	Earliest	Latest

SIZE OF FAMILY:

married couples (with husband under 35 years old) with more than two children living at home	28.8 (1960)	19.8 (1972)
adults desiring families with four or more children	49 (1945)	20 (1973)

RESIDENTIAL ISOLATION:

occupied dwelling units having just one occupant	9.3 (1950)	15 (1965)
occupied dwelling units in which none of the occupants are related	10 (1948)	18 (1968)

DIVORCE:

divorced persons in the population (14 years old and older)		
men	1.8 (1955)	2.2 (1966)
women	2.3 (1955)	3.1 (1966)

Notes (refer to references at back of paper)
Children in single-parent families: (32)
Married couples with no children: (33)
Households with male heads: (34)
Married couples without households: (35)
Residential telephones disconnected: (36)
Women in the labor force: (37)
Professional housekeepers: (38)
Married couples with more than two children: (39)
Adults desiring four or more children: (40)
Divorced persons in the population: (41)
Occupied dwelling units with one or more unrelated
  occupants: (42)

Size of family	high variance
Divorce	low
Residential isolation	low

The data in Figure Five, for all of these variables except for neolocality, support the hypothesis that deviation from this norm has increased significantly during the post-war period. Time series data, available for some of these indicators, shows that this increased deviation has been steady over time, in some cases dating back as far as the 1930's and in some cases accelerating markedly after 1960. (31)

I am not suggesting that the nuclear family is disintegrating, but only that a certain specific type of nuclear family is declining in the frequency of its occurrence. This specific type of nuclear family has provided, for better or worse, unambiguous answers to the following questions:

1. Who is to keep house?

2. Who is to take care of dependent children?

3. Who is to take economic responsibility for dependent children?

4. How are sex partners to be chosen?

5. How are siblings for children to be provided?

6. How is personal isolation to be prevented?

For increasing numbers of people, these questions have become dilemmas, the solutions to which are to be sought not at the level of family but at the level of community.

The simultaneous decline of housekeeping as a professional role and widespread entrance of women into the labor force has created a minor crisis around the housekeeping function. The crisis is minor because technological routinization had already eroded the housekeeping function, in many instances, to less than a full-time occupation.

Many families have been able to cope with this
problem by simply dividing housekeeping tasks
equally among all responsible members. On the
whole, the developed community builders have not
felt called upon to provide a solution to this
problem. However, some of the newer planned
residential developments in Southern California
sell a service package to new homeowners through
which some housekeeping tasks are performed by the
professional staff of the development corporation
rather than by the homeowning family.

The communes, on the other hand, have taken
radical steps to transform or abolish the full-time
housekeeper role. In some rural and most urban
communes in the sample, steps have been taken to
abolish the sexual division of labor. Cooperative
team efforts in heavy household maintenance jobs
and the rotation of regular household duties (e.g.:
meal preparation and clean-up) help to destroy the
conception of housekeeping as a discrete
occupation. But by far the most interesting
contribution of communes to the transformation of
housekeeping lies in their alteration of the
boundaries of household space itself. Two-thirds
of the communes studied transferred some part of
what is ordinarily defined as private space to the
public domain. In 65% of the communes, private
households lacked kitchens and/or bathrooms. In
8%, the notion of private space was completely
abolished or reduced to the perimeters of a shelf
and a bed.

The rural communes are particularly
interesting in this regard, since many of them
have been free to experiment with the construction
of their own domiciles, whereas urban communes have
generally had to adapt to the very limited range of
what urban architecture makes available. Many
interesting experiments have been observed, but no
clear relationship has been found between commune
longevity and spatial privacy. In about one-
quarter of the communes studied, the boundary
between public and private space was changed over
time. But some of these changes involved the
expansion of private space and some involved the
contraction of private space, and no overall trend
in one direction or the other has been observed.

Who is to take care of dependent children? Here we come to a more serious problem. The Economic Report of the President for 1973 cited lack of acceptable childcare facilities as the major obstacle keeping women who want to work out of the labor force. The demand for public child-care centers has been a cornerstone of most proposals and pilot projects for organized community, whether sponsored, aroused, developed, or intentional.

Public facilities for the care of pre-school children have been built into a number of the new comprehensive community developments. At the most famous of these communities--Columbia, Maryland, for instance:

> There is a network of child care centers where children of working mothers can be left, or where any busy wife can park a child for seventy-five cents an hour. There are village play areas where chil-dren can be left while Mother shops. And there are afterschool, supervised play areas for six-to-twelve-year-olds who have working mothers. (43)

It is interesting to note that organized day care centers have not been as popular in the communes. Both cooperative agreements and extended family arrangements were found in more cases than day care centers. Rather than asking why day care centers are relatively unpopular in communes, we might reverse the question and ask why cooperative arrangements do not suffice outside the commune. Cooperative agreements require the willingness of the participants to accept a pattern of investments and returns that balance out for the individual only in the long run. Willingness to enter into such agreements may very well be the hallmark of genuine community. As we have seen in discussing the neighborhood, the "free rider problem" in the modern community creates a reluctance on the part of many people to enter into cooperative agreements. This reluctance will be seen to exist in areas other than childrearing. Nor are the communes themselves free of this problem.

In a similar manner communes seek larger level

solutions to the other familial problems listed
above. The crucial point to realize about the
solutions attempted by both encounter groups and
communes is their mixed religio-familio-neighborly
functions. Communes and encounter groups do not
generally respect the traditional boundaries
separating religion from family, family from
neighborhood, and neighborhood from religion. This
makes them puzzling to those accustomed to thinking
in terms of the compartmentalized institutional
categories of our larger culture.

> Back (1972) raises the crucial issue
> of the relationship of sensitivity
> training to science and religion:
> "Encounter groups today perform some
> of the functions previously filled by
> religious experiences." Back also
> describes strains impinging on the group
> leader or facilitator by virtue of the
> fact that although he gives some of the
> gratifications of the religious healer,
> his claims are couched in the terminology
> of the scientist and based on the
> prestige of science in society. He
> concludes that intensive groups occupy
> an ambiguous position, frequently
> couching essentially religious experiences
> in scientific terminology, ...
> (44)

Many of Ruitenbeck's (45)   interpretations
parallel Back's descriptions of intensive groups:

> The differences between the revival
> meeting and marathon group therapy,
> the Living Theater, a weekend at one
> of the new institutes such as Esalen,
> and other forms of therapeutic encounter
> are largely limited to ideology; other-
> wise, the quality of human experience is
> markedly similar. (46)

Communes and encounter groups seek a blending
of the spiritual and familial not readily available
in our society. They seek a mode of association
whose level of intimacy is probably less than that
of the nuclear family but greater than that of most
neighborhoods. As such they are best seen as

representatives of a movement whose success in American society is by no means assured or necessarily desirable: a movement away from spontaneous residential community groupings toward restrictive grouped communities with the authority to impose patterns of cultural distinctiveness upon their members.

Although such a movement has met certain important needs for many people, in many other ways it goes against the American grain. It is therefore of some interest to discuss how such communal manifestations have thus far been received in American society.

The public is most conscious of a social movement when it is making the news. A movement makes news when it disrupts (or threatens to disrupt) the equilibrium of established social institutions. Thus, there is a misleading bias inherent in the measurement of a social movement's activities by the number of its media citations. Communes have, in fact, succeeded in reaching more of a peace with established society, creating less irritation, and thus have drawn less publicity. As communes have become less radical in their programs, less threatening in their behavior, and less shocking in their morality, they have experienced a rapid decline in newsworthiness. This has led to the impression on the part of many that communitarianism, as a lifestyle, has dwindled. This is not the case. There were probably more people living communally in 1975 than in any of the previous nine years. However, the virulence of the movement has declined greatly in these ten years.

A crude indicator of the degree to which the body politic responds to communitarianism as a virulent institution is the change in public opinion towards communal living. A study performed on a national sample of American adults* (eighteen

----

*The survey asks the following question: "Many changes have taken place in this country over the past ten years. These changes have frequently resulted from social movements of various kinds. Some of the movements and the issues raised by them have received wide support from the public.

years old and over) shows communitarianism to be a
consistently unpopular social movement (Figure
Six). The study, replicated annually since 1972,
shows a consistent pattern in American attitudes
towards a variety of social movements. Consumerism
is and has remained the most popular of these
movements. About ninety percent of the population
records favorable attitudes. Consumerism is
followed in descending order of favor by the civil
rights movement, birth control movement, women's
liberation, the movement for the legalization of
marijuana, and finally, communal living. However,
the commune movement has experienced the greatest
proportional increase, during the test year of
1974-1975 going from fourteen percent approval to
twenty-one percent approval. This increase still
left the movement slightly behind the movement for
legalization of marijuana.

Communal living is looked on more favorably
by males than by females, and more by the young
than the old. For example, only thirty-four
percent of those in the 18-24 year old bracket in
1975 were very much opposed to communal living
whereas seventy percent of those in the 45-54 year
old bracket were so opposed. In general,
opposition to communal living increased steadily
with increasing age. Surprisingly, in view of
their virtual absence from the communal living
scene, non-whites have been more favorably disposed
to communal living than whites. This, however,
may reflect the generally more positive attitudes
towards social movements of non-whites as compared
to whites, and may be a spill-over effect from the
vastly more favorable attitude of non-whites
towards the civil rights movement in the last four
years. The racial pattern of communal living held
for all of the other social movements except for
consumerism.

Others have been less popular. We are interested
in your own opinions. For each of these
movements and/or issues I mention, tell me whether
you are completely for it, more for it than
against, more against it than for it, or completely
against it." (47)

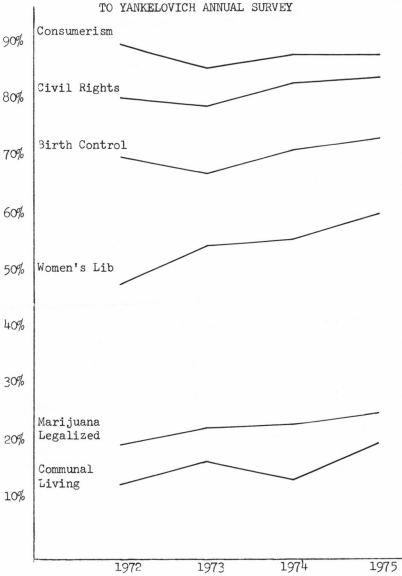

FIGURE 6
ATTITUDES TOWARDS SOCIAL MOVEMENTS - ANNUALLY SINCE 1972
PROPORTION FAVORABLE TO EACH MOVEMENT ACCORDING
TO YANKELOVICH ANNUAL SURVEY

Mutual Causation in the Development of
Communes and Encounter Groups

We have now come as far as we can operating
under the simplifying assumption that communes and
encounter groups are part of one monolithic social
movement. A strong case for such a monolithic
approach has been made by Marx and Ellison:

> The linkage between sensitivity
> training and communes is made explicit
> in Jacobs' article on "Emotive
> and Control Groups as Mutated New
> American Utopian Communities." She
> proposes that all utopias provide both
> controls and support for individuals
> not found elsewhere:
>
>> Homologies to utopian communitarian
>> thought and practice now exist in
>> the contemporary proliferating
>> control and emotive groups, which
>> range from group therapy to encounter
>> groups, T-groups, "Rap" groups,
>> growth and human relations centers,
>> etc. The ideology of these groups
>> and the expectation from them relates
>> as much to the utopian tradition and
>> to the social tensions which create
>> and popularize all utopian movements
>> as to the psychoanalytical or other
>> psychological movements from which
>> they are usually considered derived . . .
>> in their pure type, these groups
>> function like all utopias which seek
>> to compensate for self-difficulties
>> in a culture.
>
> Like Ruitenbeck, Jacobs emphasizes the
> quasi-religious characteristics and
> sources of the group movement. This
> leads her to conceive of intensive groups
> as "part-time quasi-communities." The
> early utopian period of the group
> movement was characterized by testimonials
> to the recuperative value and therapeutic
> benefits of participation in intensive
> groups. In the later and current period,
> involvement and participation in intensive
> groups becomes a permanent life-style and

one becomes a long-term, part-time
member of a quasi-community. . . .
Moreover, the fact that both movements
attack a publicly sacred institution
--namely, marriage and the nuclear
family--also reflects their profound
disagreement with dominant structural
arrangements and cultural norms. (48)

Although the two movements have much in
common, it would be a mistake to neglect historical
and cultural differences in their origins and
development. Encounter groups are a much more
recent phenomenon than communes. In fact the
latter have a history which can be traced almost to
the beginning of American colonial settlement.

Communes have been in existence for a long
time. However, they have always been a peripheral
rather than central part of any known civilization.
For thousands of years, both in Asia and the West,
the communitarian impetus has never succeeded in
either catching on or dying out. John Bennett
(49)   calls it "the oldest 'new' and the most
traditional 'experimental' social movement in the
West." An ancient Oriental communitarian history
is based upon evidence clouded in myth. Some
scholars believe that self-sufficient Taoist
communes existed in China in the Fifth Century B.C.
(50). It is possible that communitarian
ashram villages existed in India even before that.
However, a well substantiated Western tradition
of communitarianism begins in the First Century
B.C.; ". . . with the Galilean withdrawal
sectarians--the Essenes and others, who . . .
sought to escape the alienation and corruption of
Roman Palestine." (51)

Communes have also existed in America since
the Seventeenth Century. The movement has burst
forth, become eclipsed, and then burst forth again
from time to time. Beginning in 1965 the
communitarian tendency that had been dormant in
American society for more than a half a century
began to show itself once again.

The American communitarian movement of 1965-
1975 started at the Atlantic and Pacific coasts
and moved inland. As with any blanket statement

about the origin of a social movement, this one is
something of an oversimplification. Survivals of
communitarian movements from earlier in the century
still were to be found in the Sierra Nevadas, the
Appalachians, and the Ozark mountain regions in the
early 1960's, and these had a minor but not
insignificant part in the development of contemporary communitarianism. There exist records of
hippie-like communes in San Francisco and New York
as early as 1963, although even in these cities
nothing approximating a social movement got started
until 1965.

Tens of thousands of communes, both rural and
urban, have come into being in the United States
between the years of 1965 and 1975 and beyond
(52).   Most of these have been extremely short-
lived, lasting no more than two or three years.
Communes are distinctive among the alternative
lifestyles, both in the tremendous variety of
alternatives that have been experimented with and
in the degree of divergence from modal patterns of
valuation which the isolation and mutual reinforcement of communal living make possible. Zablocki
(53)   with respect to the Bruderhof, and
Bugliosi (54),   with respect to the Manson
family, both indicate how lifestyles almost
totally alien to the values accepted as normal by
the larger society can be successfully maintained
over an extended period of time in a small,
enclosed group setting. Control of boundaries
and renunciation of external social ties are among
the commitment mechanisms that Kanter (55)   found
differentiated long-lived from short-lived
communities in the past. Bettelheim (56),   in his
analysis of the Israeli kibbutzim, also stresses
the importance of isolation for the maintenance of
such widely divergent lifestyles. He points out
that kibbutzim have not existed in Israeli cities
and comments that "Kibbutzim can exist only (it
seems) if the group life is not interfered with by
meeting nongroup members at every step."
Berger and Hackett (57)   have argued that while
communal living has been identified with the
radical political philosophies of the new left
during the 1960's, "there is a sense in which the
more serious rural communards, despite their
apparent total rejection of middle-class industrial
styles of life, may be said to be conservative in
the sense that this term is sometimes applied to

rural or small-town folk who resist the
technological incursions of modernity
Kanter (58)   has made a similar point in arguing
that communal living of the 1960's and 1970's,
unlike its analogue in the nineteenth century, has
been oriented towards the structuring of alternative families rather than alternative societies.

There is no historical analogue for the
development of encounter groups, a relatively
recent phenomenon. As Marx and Ellison have
pointed out:

In one form or another, laboratory
training approaches in human relations
have been around since 1947 when three
social psychologists founded the
National Training Laboratories (NTL)
as well as the social movement that has
come to be associated with the term
"sensitivity training." Nevertheless,
the movement only exploded in popularity
and notoriety within the past ten years.
And this explosion has been a result of
the emergence of "personal growth" or
"encounter" groups, approaches, and
techniques. The unprecedented growth
in the popularity of intensive groups
suggests that this phenomenon constitutes
a major social movement in contemporary
American society. . . . Group approaches
have greatest appeal to people under 40
and are organized by practitioners who
are relatively youthful compared to
professionals in related fields.
(59)

Although encounter groups have been around
for at least three decades and communes for many
times that number, it is only in the decade 1965-
1975 that it would have occurred to anyone to
juxtapose the two phenomena. This juxtaposition
is a two-way street. Encounter group attempters
are well aware of the similarity of their goals
to those of communes members and vice versa. Marx
and Ellison (60)   quote Howard as observing:

Esoteric veterans of the human
potential movement talk of founding
communes and kibbutzim -- isolated

country retreats where honesty and
openness can prevail. (Doctor Frederick
Perls has founded a commune in British
Columbia; Philip Slater of Brandeis
University said he hoped to start one
of his own.) A less exotic manifestation
of the widespread longing for 'community'
is the neighborhood T-group.

A study which I have recently completed using
the sample of 120 contemporary rural and urban
communes indicated that more than half of these
have had encounter group experience (see Figure
Seven). Most of those with such experience had it
prior to joining the commune. Unfortunately, no
control group comparisons exist for the general
population. However, I think it would be justified
to infer commune members have a significantly
greater than average likelihood of having had
previous exposure to encounter groups.

The data from the above mentioned study (61)
also indicate a connection in the opposite
direction--a high degree of communal interest in
encountering techniques. As Figure Eight indicates,
this tendency for communes to utilize encountering
techniques as part of their communal life is much
more pronounced for rural than for urban communes.
We may therefore provisionally conclude that there
is some degree of mutual interrelationship between
the encounter group movement and the commune
movement and that both certainly draw from a
similar restricted pool of potential recruits.

The differences between communes and encounter
groups are also quite pronounced. Marx and
Ellison (62)   summarize some of these differences
as follows:

This interpretation is not super-
ficially obvious. In fact, the
differences between contemporary communes
and sensitivity training groups are,
on the surface, quite blatant. For
example, communards generally intend to
establish (at least relatively) permanent
collectivities. In contrast, intensive
groups begin with an explicitly limited
life-span--even though some groups extend
far beyond this initially-established

FIGURE 7

Social Diversity of Members' Experiences
Before and After Joining Commune

CHARACTERISTIC		Before	After	Never	N
Yoga		39.9%	34.3%	50.2%*	542
By Sex:	Male	38.2	34.2	51.3	298
	Female	41.8	34.4	48.8	244
Group Psychotherapy		23.8	17.3	66.6	542
By Sex:	Male	26.5	18.8	62.4	298
	Female	20.5	15.6	71.7	244
Individual Psychotherapy		29.2	12.6	64.9	**542**
By Sex:	Male	27.2	9.4	67.4	298
	Female	31.5	16.4	61.9	244
Consciousness Raising Group		39.9	36.4	46.1	542
By Sex:	Male	38.9	38.6	46.0	298
	Female	41.0	33.6	46.3	244
Encounter or Sensitivity Training		41.0	24.9	47.6	542
By Sex:	Male	42.3	23.2	48.3	298
	Female	39.3	27.0	46.7	244

*Note that all rows add up to more than 100% be-
cause those respondents reporting the experience
both before and after joining are counted in both
of these columns.

FIGURE 8

FREQUENCY OF COMMITMENT
INDUCING RITUALS IN COMMUNAL LIFE

Collective Rituals (Total # engaging is in parenthesis)	Proportion of Communes Engaging in the Ritual	
	Urban (N=60)	Rural (N=60)
Meditation (63)	27%	79%
Prayer (36)	18%	42%
Mutual Criticism (32)	18%	34%
Yoga (31)	12%	40%
Shared Silence (30)	17%	33%
Drug Ingestion (23)	13%	25%
Singing (19)	22%	10%
Group Readings (19)	12%	7%
Chanting Mantras (16)	5%	22%
Dancing (13)	7%	15%
Group Confession (12)	7%	13%
Group Sex (8)	2%	12%
Contact w/Spirits (7)	10%	1%
Speaking in Tongues (6)	3%	7%

limit and become semi-permanent
collectivities. Furthermore, communal
membership is relatively inclusive
and continuous (even when jobs are held
outside the commune, a practice which is
becoming increasingly frequent as urban-
metropolitan communes proliferate), rather
than sporadic, isolated and compartmentalized. Most communards spend a
large proportion of their daily time,
energy, and significant activities within
the commune. In contrast, intensive
groups meet sporadically and for limited
time periods. Finally, communes generally
imply sharing--of political and socio-
economic perspectives, if not of income,
wealth, and property as well. Sensitivity
training groups imply no such material or
attitudinal sharing--other than the sharing
of personal-emotional intimacies.

What distinguishes the two is the kind of investment which individuals are prepared to make in a
voluntary communal collectivity. In order to
provide what I believe to be a productive framework
for viewing these investment differences, we must
distinguish between two types of investment:
investment of resources and investment of self.

Let the self be defined, operationally, as
that entity on behalf of which choices are made.
The individual can identify with larger social
entities wholly or in part. We shall refer to such
identifications as "investments of self." An
investment of self into a corporate actor shall
be considered an assignment, to that corporate
actor (or some agent thereof), of some degree of
power to shape the preferences of the given
individual. An individual invests some portion of
his "self" into a corporate actor in the hope that
the corporate actor will be able to use its
preference shaping powers to achieve consensus to
take action that will benefit the individual more
than the individual could have been benefited by
retaining preference autonomy and taking action on
his own. Investment of self is equivalent, in game
theoretic terms, to the entries in the payoff
matrix being functions of exogenous variables.

Because of the high degree of risk involved
in the investment of self, this phenomenon is most
often found in association with religious or
utopian movements or life and death situations
such as combat in war. Many of the mechanisms of
preference modification therefore are derived from
religious literature. I will discuss three such
mechanisms here: sacrifice, renunciation, and
mortification.*

Sacrifice may be defined as the act of
investment of resources into a group beyond what
would be justified by rational calculation of
expected return on the investment, in the hope of
stimulating a similar increase in commitment by
others. Renunciation may be defined as the
voluntary reduction of possible orderings in one's
preference set (what Sen (63) and others have
referred to as value restrictiveness) in order to
help bring about coherence in the collective
choice. It is typical of religious communities
that they demand during the period of novitiate
extreme curtailment of the admissible orderings in
the novice's preference sets, even with regard
to inconsequential or trivial decisions (64).
This is a form of discipline to assure that such
groups, which typically require unanimity for
decision making, will always be able to bring the
preferences of their members into sufficient
harmony with respect to important issues in the
future. Finally, mortification can be defined as
the direct submission of the orderings of one's
preferences to social control. Mortification is
typically a gruelling psychological process, often
requiring the physical and/or mental and emotional
torture of the participant.

Weber distinguishes between associative
groups and communal groups on the basis of the
source of motivation for commitment: rational or
emotional. Such a formulation precludes the
possibility of developing rational models to
account for behavior in any but associational
collectivities. Indeed, there have been few
attempts, perhaps for this reason, to account for

---

*These three have been identified as commitment
mechanisms in 19th century utopian communities.
(65)

the behavior of people in crowds, communities,
etc. in terms of a rational model of behavior.
But our formulation suggests the possibility of
defining a typology of collectivities in terms of
investment criteria, such that the possibility
of applying a general rational model is not
precluded.

FIGURE 9

INVESTMENT OF RESOURCES

		YES	NO
INVESTMENT OF SELF	YES	COMMUNITY (unity)*	CROWD (homogeneity)*
	NO	ASSOCIATION (unanimity)*	ASSEMBLY (uniformity)*

*basis for consensus

In Figure Nine, such a typology is put forth.
Collectivities may be distinguished solely in
terms of the investments of their participants.
The associational group is thus defined, not as
the rational groups, but as that collectivity in
which members invest of their resources but not of
themselves. The crowd is defined as a collectivity
in which self is invested without resources, thus
accounting for the instability of such entities
and the efficacy of visible gestures of sacrifice
(e.g., in combat) in transforming crowds into
communities. The community is defined as that
type of collectivity in which members invest both
self and resources. The assembly is a residual
category applying to collectivities of those who
happen to converge in time and space but with no
investment of any kind being given.

The encounter group may then be defined as a
kind of crowd. More stable, of course, than mobs

or rioting groups, the encounter group is nevertheless characterized by individual investment of
self without concomitant investment of resources.

It may seem paradoxical to assert that
communes foster both the quest for solitude and
the quest for total immersion of the self into the
collectivity. But these two contraries are united
in their opposition to the self. Schachter (66)
brings the two together under the concept of
deindividuation. His review of much literature
on both voluntary and coerced isolation indicates
that the result of isolation is not the enhance-
ment but the destruction of the self:

> When the great resolution has been taken,
> to leave all and go in search of God
> in solitude, there comes that first-hour
> zest which attends all new undertakings
> begun with good will. That lasts as long
> as it ought to last; more shortly for
> big souls, longer for the lesser--it is
> the jam to get the powder down. Then begins
> the first revelation, and a very unpleasant
> one it is. The solitary begins to see
> himself as he really is. The meanness,
> the crookedness of natural character begins
> to stand out in a strong light; those
> wounds that disobedience to conscience in
> the past has left festering, now give forth
> their poisoned matter. (67)

Moreover, Schachter, following Festinger, et
al., (68) distinguishes two classes of needs
which group membership satisfies. The first are
needs for evaluation which require that the
individual remain distinct from the group. But
the other are needs for deindividuation, in which
the individual loses personal responsibility for
his actions:

> It is suggested that there are many
> kinds of behavior in which the individual
> would like to engage where activity is
> prevented by the existence of inner
> restraints. Instances of such behavior
> might be acting wildly and boisterously,
> "talking dirty," expressing hostilities,

and so on. Festinger et al. suggest
that under conditions where the
individual is not "individuated" in
a group, such restraints will be
reduced and individuals will be able
to satisfy needs which might otherwise
remain unsatisfied. In an ingenious
experiment, these authors demonstrate
that the state of deindividuation in
the group does occur and is accompanied
by reduction of the inner restraints
of the members of the group. Further,
they demonstrate that groups in which
such restraints are reduced are more
attractive to their members than groups
in which restraints are not reduced.
(69)

Both the quest for solitude and the quest for
deindividuation have been associated, throughout
history and in many cultures, with certain
mechanisms which loosen the association between
person and self. Some of these mechanisms may be
found in the organization of communal households.

Because the personal self constantly seeks
to reassert itself, the closest that communes can
come to stable equilibrium is the achievement of
periodic renewal through institutionalized
communion. One mechanism of this is through drugs:

Many of the contemporary communitarians
have sought communion in drugs. In
fact, the drug scene first emerged in
the early 1960's in communal groups in
California and on the East Coast. Why
was it a key element in so many communes
only to disappear as the groups matured?
Largely because the attempts to break
down the barriers between people our
alienating culture has erected required,
in the heat of the 1960's, drastic
methods. The communitarians sought
instant communication, the group soul,
and drugs helped. But drugs soon became
a liability, because they sabotaged the
vital instrumental fabric, the life-
sustaining activities. In drugs, the
commune cannot find a permanent existence,
and especially a model for either individual

or social reconstruction. Still,
the drugs played their role, and led to
ingenious new symbols and group
associations. (70)

The alteration of consciousness in communion
leads to an increase in charismatic susceptibility.
There is an absorption of intimate feelings by
the charismatic leader and the entire collectivity.
But renewal will not result unless the investment
of self, on the part of each individual, is thereby achieved. Under ordinary circumstances, two
identical experiences of alteration of consciousness may give rise--one to renewal, the other to
malaise.

This is what is so sad. When you take money
out of the bank, when you are spending money faster
than you are earning it, your path to bankruptcy
is easy to see. But you cannot easily tell when
your social account is being depleted. Experiences
of spiritual and emotional renewal are subtle and
deceiving. Often the sheer intensity of a
renewal of solidarity is greatest as the network
of relationships is already entering its death
throes. Communal love can be a signal of communal
decay. The usual guidelines for knowing when to
work hard at relationships and when to relax do
not seem to apply to communal situations. Nobody
intuitively grasps the necessary lead times.

Despite the pitfalls, the investment of self
in communal organizations is often seen as worth-
while by the individual. As an ego-renunciation
problem it is a valid form of yoga--perhaps the
most valid for a Westerner with a sense of
political and social responsibility--the yoga of
inter-personal harmony through renunciation of
primary allegiance to the isolated ego.

Conclusion

In this paper we have discussed evidence that
encounter groups and communes are expressions of
cultural and demographic events of the decade
1965-1975. I have attempted to show that these
events, although peculiar to the decade in question
are not isolated phenomena. Rather they are part
of a trend in American society away from open and

spontaneous community and toward restrictive
purposive community. I have argued further that
community in the commonly used sense of residential
propinquity is not solely what is at issue here.
We are using the word community to refer to
experimental attempts to seek collective identity
by merging elements of family, religion, and
orthodox community. Most of these experimental
attempts, whether in the form of encounter groups,
communes, new towns, etc., will prove unstable and
rapidly disintegrate. This must be so because
we have neither a reliable body of empirical
knowledge or of traditional wisdom to guide us.
The selection of elements of religion, family, and
neighborhood to be blended must, therefore,
proceed on a trial and error basis. This paper is
not the place to evaluate what guidelines may
have emerged in the first decade of experimentation. However, the willingness of many encounter
group participants and commune members to document
their experiences--both successes and failures--
will be greatly helpful in this endeavor.

In the last part of this paper I have
attempted to lay out the beginnings of a
theoretical framework in which a wide variety of
encounter group and community experiments can be
treated. The framework is based upon this critical
assumption: the self may be considered an entity
which can be invested either in other persons or
in collectivities. The economics of self investment differ, of course, to some extent from the
economics of the investment of resources. From
this point of view, the primary distinction
between encounter groups and communes is that
encounter groups call only for the investment of
self whereas communes call for the investment of
both self and resources. In a large-scale piece
of research in progress, I have attempted to apply
this theoretical perspective to the study of a
national sample of contemporary communes.
Although the success of this theoretical perspective remains to be demonstrated, I hope that it
will provide at least the beginning of an attempt
to unify our discussion of these very important
but highly elusive phenomena.

REFERENCES

1. D. Bell, The Coming of Post-Industrial Society: A Venture in Social Forecasting (Basic Books, New York, 1973).

2. Lincoln H. Clark and Nelson N. Foote, Eds., Consumer Behavior (New York University Press, New York, 1955-1961, 4 vols.).

3. Benjamin D. Zablocki, Some Models of Commune Integration, presented at the Annual Meeting of the American Sociological Association, 1972; Benjamin D. Zablocki, Alienation and Charisma in a Context of Decision Making, presented at the Annual Meeting of the Public Choice Society Chicago, Ill., April 1975.

4. E. H. Erickson, Childhood and Society (Norton, New York, ed. 2, 1964).

5. J. S. Coleman, Youth: Transition to Adulthood (University of Chicago Press, Chicago, Ill., 1974); R. J. Havighurst and P. Dreyer, in Youth; The Seventy-Fourth Yearbook of the National Society for the Study of Education, R. J. Havighurst and P. Dreyer, Eds. (University of Chicago Press, Chicago, 1975).

6. W. J. Goode, After Divorce (Free Press, Glencoe, Ill., 1965).

7. A. R. Hochschild, The Unexpected Community (Prentice-Hall, Englewood Cliffs, N.J., 1973); A. R. Hochschild, American Sociological Review, 40, 553-69 (1975); G. F. Streib, Int. J. Psychiatry, 6, 69-76 (1968).

8. R. J. Havighurst and P. Dreyer, op. cit.

9. Paul Glick, Current Population Reports, 52, 23 (1975).

10. P. Laslett et al., Household and Family in Past Time (Cambridge U. Press, Cambridge, Mass., 1972).

11. Johnston and Herron, New York Times, September 24 (1974).

12. _____, ibid.

13. John C. Belcher, Journal of Marriage and the Family, 29, 3, 534-40 (1967).

14. Article without byline in Los Angeles Times, August 21, p. 19 (1971).

15. A. R. Hochschild, op. cit.

16. Benjamin D. Zablocki and Rosabeth Moss Kanter, Annual Review of Sociology, 2, 269-98 (1976).

17. B. M. Berger, Looking for America: Essays on Youth, Suburbia, and Other American Obsessions, (Prentice-Hall, Englewood Cliffs, N.J., 1971).

18. G. D. Suttles, The Social Construction of Communities (University of Chicago Press, Chicago, 1972), pp. 267-8.

19. J. S. Coleman, Journal of Mathematical Sociology, 1, 1-47 (1971).

20. G. D. Suttles, op. cit., p. 162.

21. J. Needleman, The New Religions (Doubleday, Garden City, N.Y., 1970).

22. J. Lofland, Doomsday Cult (Prentice-Hall, Englewood Cliffs, N.J., 1966).

23. L. Veysey, The Communal Experience (Harper & Row, New York, 1973).

24. R. Gustaitis, Turning On (Macmillan, New York, 1969).

25. George B. Leonard, The Transformation; A Guide to the Inevitable Changes in Humankind (Delacorte, New York, 1972); George B. Leonard, The Ultimate Athlete (Viking, New York, 1975).

26. A. Smith, Powers of Mind (Random House, New York, 1975).

27. A. A. Goren, The New York Jews Quest of Community: The Kahilah Experiment, 1908-1922 (Columbia University Press, New York, 1970).

28. M. Sklare, Ed., Jewish Community in America (Behrman, New York, 1974) p. 105.

29. J. Neusner, Contemporary Judaic Fellowship in Theory and in Practice (Ktav, New York, 1972).

30. Constant H. Jacquet, Jr., Statistics of Organized Religion in the U.S.: A General Appraisal (mimeographed paper, 1975).

31. Abbott Ferris, Indicators of Change in the American Family (Russell Sage Foundation, New York, 1970).

32. Urie Bronfenbrunner, Saturday Review of Education, March, 32 (1973).

33. Statistical Abstract of the United States: 1973 (United States Bureau of the Census, Washington, D.C.), p. 4.

34. Abbott Ferris, op. cit., p. 44.

35. _____, ibid., p. 35.

36. Vance Packard, A Nation of Strangers (David McKay Co., New York, 1972), p. 8.

37. Economic Report of the President: Transmitted to Congress January 1973 (U.S. Government Printing Office, Washington, D.C., 1973), p. 107.

38. D. Sragow, Civil Rights Digest, 4, 1, 34-37 (1974).

39. United States Bureau of the Census, op. cit.

40. Article without byline in Los Angeles Herald Examiner, February 5, p. 10 (1973).

41. Paul Glick and Robert Parke, Jr., in Readings on the Sociology of the Family, Bert N. Adams and Thomas Weirath, Eds. (Markham Publishing Co., Chicago, 1971), p. 454.

42. John C. Belcher, op. cit., p. 535.

43. Vance Packard, op. cit., p. 325.

44. John H. Marx and David L. Ellison, Sensitivity Training and Communes: Contemporary Quests for Community (mimeographed paper, 1973), p. 45.

45. Ruitenbeck, as quoted in John H. Marx and David L. Ellison (44).

46. John H. Marx and David L. Ellison, op. cit.

47. Current Opinion (The Roper Public Opinion Research Center, Williams College, Williamstown, Mass., Vol. II, Issue 9, September 1974), pp. 98-99.

48. John H. Marx and David L. Ellison, op. cit.

49. John W. Bennett, Theory and Society, 2, 63-94 (1975).

50. R. S. Fogarty, American Utopianism (Peacock Publications, Itasca, Ill., 1972).

51. John W. Bennett, op. cit.

52. Benjamin D. Zablocki, Alienation and Investment of Self in the Urban Commune (Project Rep. National Institute of Mental Health, Washington D.C., 1975).

53. _____, The Joyful Community (Penguin Books, Baltimore, 1971).

54. V. Bugliosi and C. Gentry, Helter Skelter: The True Story of the Manson Murders (Norton, New York, 1974).

55. Rosabeth Moss Kanter, Commitment and Community: Communes and Utopias in Sociological Perspective (Harvard University Press, Cambridge, Mass., 1972).

56. B. Bettelheim, The Children of the Dream (Avon, New York, 1969), p. 283.

57. B. M. Berger and B. M. Hackett, Journal of Sociological Issues, 30, 163-83 (1974).

58. Rosabeth Moss Kanter, op. cit.

59. John H. Marx and David L. Ellison, op. cit.

60. _____, ibid.

61. Benjamin D. Zablocki, <u>Alienation and Charisma:</u> <u>American Communitarian Experiments: 1965-1975</u> (Free Press, New York, in press).

62. John H. Marx and David L. Ellison, <u>op</u>. <u>cit</u>.

63. Amartya K. Sen, <u>Collective Choice and</u> <u>Social Welfare</u> (Holden-Day, San Francisco, 1970).

64. Benjamin D. Zablocki, <u>op</u>. <u>cit</u>., p. 251.

65. Rosabeth Moss Kanter, <u>op</u>. <u>cit</u>.

66. Stanley Schachter, <u>The Psychology of</u> <u>Affiliation; Experimental Studies of the</u> <u>Sources of Gregariousness</u> (Stanford University Press, Stanford, Cal., 1959).

67. _____, <u>ibid</u>.

68. L. Festinger <u>et al</u>., <u>Journal of Abnormal</u> <u>Social Psychology</u>, 1952.

69. Stanley Schachter, <u>op</u>. <u>cit</u>., p. 2.

70. John W. Bennett, <u>op</u>. <u>cit</u>., p. 87.

Alexander D. Blumenstiel, president of Personnel Assessment Services in Boston, is a management consultant in the areas of employee selection and promotion assessments, employee relations, and industrial relations. He has conducted extensive research and authored numerous publications in social psychology, management, and laboratory training.

6

Sensitivity Training:
Dilemmas in Paradise

Alexander D. Blumenstiel

Introduction

A curious notion once captured the efforts of surprising
numbers of people: temporarily freeing communication between
people from the constraints, threats and tensions of everyday life promises the fulfillment of a universal dream--
RELIEF. Relief, that is, from a major portion of man's
inescapable social and psychological troubles.

A curious notion once captured the efforts of surprising
numbers of other people (though there was a highly significant overlap in the membership of both groups) that the
effects of this freedom could be scientifically studied and
validated, or invalidated as the case may be. I was once a
member of the latter group.

In later days, the notion and the efforts I've referred
to in my first paragraph, above, became known as the
"Encounter Movement" and well known variants of this label.

The efforts referred to in the second paragraph above
are still, typically, known as "behavioral science."

In a period extending from 1966 through 1970, as a
behavioral scientist, I performed a number of studies of one
facet of the Encounter Movement--Sensitivity Training.
Sensitivity Training is a term generic to a therapeutic
effort sponsored, largely, by the National Training
Laboratories, and its associated organizations. In fact,
demonstrative of the relationship between practitioners and
researchers, my research was supported, in large part, by the
NTL.

In spite of this support (which was, in fact, free from
attempts to pressure me in any way), eventually my conclusion

about both Sensitivity Training and the Encounter Movement
was largely negative. I didn't see what good it did, could
do, or might do. And, in any case, I didn't see any way in
which honest validity studies could be performed to test it
out.

I wasn't alone in this conclusion, though it didn't do
my professional career much good to state it as often as I
did, at the time.

Since the early seventies, however, things have changed.
For one, the Sensitivity Training-Encounter Movement has
fallen on bad times, as has so much else. For another, I've
mellowed and now do not think it was so bad a thing, provable
or not.

The paper I initially presented as part of the symposium
at the 1971 meetings of the AAAS was predicated upon earlier
opinions of mine and was offered in a context of much stronger support for Sensitivity than now exists. Sensitivity
Trainers, at the time, were drawing good consulting fees,
even though the handwriting on the wall was darkening. Their
struggle to prove validity was, I think, a reaction to this
darkening. An I think it is now time to give up the struggle
and to accept Sensitivity Training for what it was, and may
yet be.

Sensitivity Training, the way I now see it, was a lovely
escape into human tenderness and intimacy made available to
people who ordinarily didn't have the opportunity to enjoy the
warmth of relatively unrestrained interaction with others.
Luckily, in the sixties and early seventies, the people who
needed this escape were in a position to be able to afford it.
I'm not so sure they still can. And it's a pity.

As far as the behavioral science effort to document
effects attributable to "change" in people from participation
in training laboratories is concerned, however, I still think
it laughable. Not only have validity studies proven nothing,
as far as I know, but they make the whole thing ludicrous.
Trying to prove that Sensitivity Training does good is like
trying to prove that love does good. The fact of the matter
is that of course it does good! Of course it makes people
"better"! How could it do otherwise? It is the essence of
"good" and "betterness" itself! Offered in a context which
makes it acceptable to people who would otherwise shun it.

Trying to prove this, however, is like trying to prove
that one person is better than another; like trying to prove

that it is better to live than to die; that it is better to
be a child than an adult, or vice versa. The question, itself, might be seen as part of an advertising rhetoric that,
unfortunately, did in the thing it was supposed to sell.

Today, the Movement is not doing well. I think this is
is due to a number of reasons. First, things are much more
basic today than they were in its heyday. The struggle for
survival is more acute and Sensitivity Training is a frill
few can afford. It used to be a reasonable business expense,
for example, because executives felt it might do some good
and make people generally happier in their work. But, since
you can't easily document that it improves the profit
picture and since that bottom line is much more critical
today than ten years ago, happiness in work has to be
determined in much more certain ways--by better employee
selection procedures, for instance.

Second, as I indicated above, the effort to prove
validity had the opposite effect. It showed that you can't
prove the validity of an essentially social movement. But
it also made a lot of potential customers concerned about
validity. And, since it couldn't be demonstrated, they were
turned off.

Third, people who did go through training laboratories
are not in the market for more. They have gone on to other
things: retirement, raising families, psychotherapy, etc.
Social movements phase in and out. Their ethos, or essential
message takes different forms.

Sensitivity is still a valuable commodity, however,
perhaps needed more today than before. And there is no doubt
that Sensitivity Training was a wonderful experience for many
of those who got it. If only we could still afford it...
Because it was valid as a search for community, whatever its
scientific merits. And we need community more than ever.

I've had to work my original paper over considerably
for this published volume, though some of my original
cynicism probably still shows through. The remainder of this
essay describes some of the features of Sensitivity Training
Laboratories I attended in the role of observer and some of
my ideas about why people in them felt the way they did.

It's Like a Vacation

One of the reasons, I think, why people did, in fact,
achieve a degree of intimacy in communication with others in
Sensitivity Training Laboratories which is not as often the

case elsewhere is because they felt good about being in the
Laboratory situation. They felt at ease, relaxed, and an
enjoyment at being with each other. Above all, they felt
like they belonged.

The basis for this is rather straightforward and almost
obvious. Most training laboratories were held at resorts or
at other places which mightily resembled them. People felt
like they were on vacation, even if there was a schedule to
keep and definite activities they were obliged to participate
in. They felt this way even though, often, they were on
company time and had been sent by the boss.

Let's take one laboratory, by way of example. We'll
call it "Woodlands" and I attended it in 1966. Woodlands was
held at a small western college in southern Utah, at the foot
of what I still think is one of the most spectacular of the
mountain areas of our country. The town was in desert, the
reds and sandstone pinks glaringly brilliant in the heat of
day. Towering immediately above it, a peak of 10,800 feet
threw dark shadows over the tableland. To say the least, it
was an imposing location and unusual enough to many of the
laboratory participants from urban areas for them to often
remark that they felt the great weight of civilization lifted
from their shoulders. There was an awe and excitment many
shared. A simple rapture created by the scene.

The winding drive through the fields of flowers and pine
forests, around wild and unbelievably striking canyons and
past extensive vistas of untracked wilderness to the topmost
bluffs was especially beautiful at dusk, when deer grazed in
the meadows close to the road. One main event during the
early days of the laboratory--which lasted two weeks--was a
cook-out at a lodge on this mountain side. What splendid
isolation! What romance! Even I, the "observer," fell in
love! Even the most fleeting flirtation seemed to portend
a new life and unparalleled rediscovery of self.

Of course, it's hard to describe in words the feeling
all this elicited. But anyone who's taken a good vacation
should understand it. It was wonderful just being there. A
very good time.

Woodlands was held in late summer; there were no
students on the campus, the mood lazy and relaxed, no bustle
nor rush and nothing much to do, except enjoy the scenery
and get Sensitivity.

Here's another example, a laboratory I went to in 1966,
as well. I call it "Executive" because the participants were

all mid-career vice-presidents from conglomerates, with a couple of middle-industry entrepreneurs who were treating themselves to the experience.

The setting for Executive was one of the most luxurious Midwestern resort hotels, in the Ozarks. Its brochure proclaimed it the "convention center of the midwest" and advertised it as providing "a unique warmness that readily lends itself to meaningful business gatherings." There was every activity imaginable, from golf to bowling. It was a middle-class paradise and I had a great time there, as did all the others.

Of course, both Woodlands and Executive seem, in retrospect, rather ritzy. Not all Sensitivity training laboratories were so high class. For instance, while I was on the faculty of Boston University, their Human Relations Center sponsored a couple of studies of larboratories they ran at the University's conference center at Osgood Hill in North Andover, a fairly rural suburb of Boston. These laboratories were for teachers, professors, health-care paraprofessionals, welfare workers, students and the like and Osgood Hill is not a great resort and North Andover is not southern Utah.

But, Osgood Hill is still impressive. It's a millionaire's summer home, a veritable Victorian castle on the crest of a hill overlooking miles of rolling New England countryside. The main house is a fine example of wainscoted and fireplaced grand fashion.

The mood at Osgood Hill was the same as at Woodlands and Executive.

Of course, many business conferences are held at such places, not just Sensitivity Training Laboratories. But the point is that they are held there for the same reasons. And there is a validity to those reasons. Such places make people feel relaxed and comfortable together and those are valuable feelings, both for Sensitivity Training and for life in general.

I don't want to belabor the obvious with this point, but I used to find it remarkable that, in all the studies of laboratory training, and with all the efforts to determine the effects of various training strategies and procedures, this fundamental decision of the movement is slighted: the initial decision to make the training laboratory, if not always then most frequently, take place apart from everyday life; in essence, the decision to make it like a vacation.

This decision, of course, has some serious consequences as far as tax deductions for business expenses are concerned, and the like. I do not mean to imply that Sensitivity Training was, or is, a vacation treated by artifice as a business expense. But, perhaps the fear that it would be so treated is one reason why closer examinations and analyses of these factors haven't been done.

The success of a training laboratory depends, however, on people opening up to each other and being frankly honest. There are many obstacles to this happening, both in everyday life and in a Sensitivity Training laboratory. In the laboratories I attended, a great deal of effort, planning and practice went into removing the barriers to interpersonal honesty and close communication. The entire notion of "training" can be seen as the effort to accomplish this.

I think the locales in which these laboratories were held were very important in helping people overcome their inhibitions to deal closely, honestly and intimately with each other in their communications. I think these locales are important for this reason in general. And I think the shame of our current situation is that the cost of using them is making them more and more unavailable to people who need them, both for Sensitivity Training and for other reasons, as well.

Who's Boss?

Modern management, informed as it is by both the philosophical underpinning of the Protestant Ethic and the functional liberalism of social science, creates something of a dilemma. This dilemma is created anew in every situation of authority and the people involved typically feel very keenly that it is a personal problem of theirs. Yet it is the old problem of human relations: simply stated, "Who's Boss?"

In Sensitivity Training laboratories, technically speaking there are no bosses. There are "participants" and there is a staff. The former are there, supposedly, voluntarily. The latter are there because they are earning satisfying consulting fees and because they like the work.

Were sensitivity training laboratories in fact vacations, problems of conflicting authority would be easily resolved - participants would do whatever they wished and the staff would either facilitate that or quit or be fired. However, because sensitivity training is supposed to be therapeutic, and because the staff are the ones who, on the surface, seem responsible for making it so, the authority picture is not that clear-cut. It's not a matter of either/or. And, because of this, participants and staff do confront some of the central problems of modern management and of human relations.

In all of the laboratories I observed, the problem of staff authority and responsibility versus participant expectations and rights was the central issue. And it was an issue that was never resolved; that is, nobody ever came to satisfactory conclusions, or resolved the dilemma.

Staff was consistently confused about its role. Participants were confused, annoyed, resigned and only fleetingly accepting of the position of staff members. And it was never clear just who was running things.

This, however, is just the way it was supposed to be. The designers of Sensitivity Training had it in mind that this very confusion would make for a situation in which the participants would be forced to "work through" their authority problems.

For example, even though the NTL staff have planning meetings before laboratories begin, even though essential decisions are made, even though the staff often meet together several days in advance to work out issues and to plan a schedule--even though this planning does take place-- when participants arrive to begin the laboratory, it suddenly seems like very little has actually been decided in advance.

For example, at Woodlands, the Community Development laboratory was planned, from before participants arrived, to force the formulation of a "community strucutre." The staff arranged for meetings, different kinds of group situations, analysis sessions, etc. And then, when participant got there, it was announced that every part of the community structure was to be produced by them and not planned by the staff. I found this confusing, as did many of the participants when they discovered that they had to spontaneously attend meetings and sessions according to a pre-arranged schedule. Also, during the first meeting, the staff announced that they hadn't really planned a role for themselves and that how the participants "used" them was up to the group. (The latter term - the group - always seemed to have an occult connotation.)

They then claimed that the only thing imposed upon both participants and staff was that they had to spend many hours a day with each other for two weeks - thus removing necessity from the schedule   they had so conscientiously arranged.

This give and take of authority characterized every
sensitivity training laboratory I attended. At the time,
I admit I had some trouble understanding it. It was very
hard for me to see just what was being accomplished and why
people were willing to bear all the confusion. My only
excuse for not understanding it at the time was that I was
a research behavioral scientist and expected it to make some
functional sense. In retrospect, it doesn't make functional
sense; it just makes common sense. It was a slice of life.

Staff members, of course, were not being paid to be
bosses. In the real world of money and status, a high
percentage of the participants could have bought and sold the
major portion of the staff members, with relatively little
effort or expense. Staff members were consultants who, in
the little fabrication of a sensitivity training scene, were
granted the privileged positions of learned major domos
required to innocuously supervise the social and emotional
play of the situation. Though they were supposed to be in
control, of course in fact they were working for the
participants. Regardless of their professionalism, their
work at planning the laboratory, their inside knowledge,
their semblence of authority, their bread was buttered by
the participants (the clients). And this, I am sure had
something to do with the democracy they tried to direct.

Thus the management dilemma which was played out in the
sensitivity training laboratory wasn't a "real" one. Staff
never were the bosses and everybody knew it. But the roles
did permit the play of the dilemma to occur. And, I suppose
people learned more about it in the process.

However, whether or not this model of human relations
based upon a dilemma of authority is actually the best one
to base a community structure on was never proven, never has
been proven, and I don't think ever will be proven. Either
you like it, or you don't. It's a question of values.

Who's Professional?

An abiding issue for behavioral and social scientists
is convincing other people that they are, by training and
skill, rightful professionals. Academic behavioral and
social scientists have never come to a satisfactory answer
to the question: Are we professionals or not? Doctors and
lawyers are professionals. Are professors? Are consultants?
Are scientists? Are Sensitivity Trainers?

Most academic social and behavioral scientist don't
really have to answer this question. So they continue to
toss it around with their usual friviolity. They are paid,
after all, to be teachers. Everybody knows what teachers
do, so it doesn't really matter if they call themselves
professionals or not.

It's a different story with consultants, however,
because being able to claim professionalism is a valuable
advertising ploy. Whatever the actual value of their
services to others, professionals are accorded a certain
respect and a right to professional fees. Professional
fees, unlike "prices," are supposed to be set in terms of
the costs of the services provided, not in terms of what the
market will bear. Nor are fee structures supposed to be
determined through market considerations. Hence, they
aren't manipulated for the sake of attraction, as are
prices. For example, a professional fee may be $100.00,
but not $99.95.

Sociologists have analyzed the "meaning" of professionalism up and down, mostly, I suspect, because they are
bothered by whether or not it applies to them. Business
consultants are paid for services rendered to clients who
are perfectly able to decide for themselves about their
value. Academics, on the other hand, are paid by a school,
not by their adolescent students.

The staff of a training laboratory is paid by NTL.
But NTL is directly concerned about the continued market-
ability of its services. Hence, it's directly important to
the staff that they have a professional image. And it is
important that the participants in a laboratory believe in
that image.

And that is the problem. For several reasons. First,
many of the staff are academics who are confused about the
meaning of professionalism as it may or may not apply to
them. Second, many of the services they render to participants are heuristic. That is, it is supposed to be a
situation in which participants are "learners." The degree
to which staff members are professionals, therefore, in many
cases, seemed to depend upon the degree of control they
appeared to exercise over the learning process. Since that
often seemed to be a very minor degree, their professional
status was often very questionable.

Participants often asked: "Just what are these guys
(staff) doing, anyway?"

And, just as often, the staff couldn't tell them.
Because it often seemed, to everybody, that the staff was, in
fact, doing nothing.

As one staff member put it: "You don't talk about what
what you are going to do. You can't."

Yet, staff members, on the whole, do believe that they
are actually doing something for the participants that the
latter can't do for themselves. And they believe that they
have to believe that they do have a professional role.

As the same staff member put it: "You know, it's really
screwy, being in a ... teaching relationship. You know you
have to believe that you have something to teach and you
have to want to teach it. So you have to believe that you
have some skills to help and that you really want to help
people. And if you begin to have doubts about it you can't
help. In other words, people can't respond to you in that
way."

Sensitivity training staff are in a very tricky position.
They must be allowed to be professional if they are to be
effective. Yet a lot of what they do seems to be nothing.
And, in general, professionals are people who take action to
help others. They don't do nothing.

So, the issue comes down to: What is nothing? A
sensitivity training group "usually begins with the withdrawal of the expected directive leadership, agenda, power
and status." (Argyris, 1966:10).

In other words, a sensitivity training group begins with
nothing. The trainer (staff member) doesn't do anything. He
just sits. Participants fidgit and ask, "Why isn't this guy
doing anything." They conclude that he doesn't know what to
do and that they are just wasting their time.

Therefore Two Predominant Dilemmas About Sensitivity Training Emerge To Devastate its Marketability

1. Undue attention drawn to the issue of validity has
never been resolved positively with an acceptable demonstra-
tion of validity. In other words, people actually being
helped by sensitivity training is a matter of hearsay and
personal testimony.

2. The professionalism of the staff is highly
questionable because, on the surface, they don't seem to do
professional things. And they, themselves, don't understand

what being professional means.

The first dilemma, I think, will never be resolved in a satisfactory manner no matter how many validity studies are done.

Trainers have made a valiant effort to resolve the second dilemma. This, successfully or not, they have done by establishing a rhetoric of professionalism which, believable or not, they have used to try to establish their legitimacy. By legitimacy, I mean deserving to be paid for what you do. Trainers claim they deserve to be paid.

And they claim a lot more.

What Trainers Claim

Trainers, generally, claim to be practicing behavioral science. They refer to theories, perspectives, orientations and research findings from behavioral sciences: psychology, sociology, social psychology, etc. This mix is characterized as "applied behavioral science." And a specialized literature has developed which details the theories, perspectives, orientations, etc., which comprise its corpus.

Trainers claim that they are learned in this corpus and that their learning, plus the apprenticeship they have served and their experience in practicing Sensitivity Training, qualifies them to practice their profession.

Now, as it happens, I think they are right. They do have valuable knowledge, they are experienced (for the most part), and they are qualified (by NTL). They do deserve to be paid for their work, and paid well.

But they have also established an unfortunate rhetoric in order to defend their legitimacy which is entirely unnecessary, excessively wordy, and gets in their way.

It is a rhetoric of the worst sort. A pseudoprofessional, academic, trite and meaningless, jargonistic rhetoric which combines the factuousness of the social sciences with a mushy sentimentalism.

The following two quotes are examples of this. They speak (or, as the case may be, don't speak) for themselves.

"Each person is limited by his own acquired and changing trust boundary. The trainer learns to be as loving as <u>he</u> can be--as accepting as his level of personal growth permits.

He must learn how trusting he is able to be in all groups
and in each special group. As he becomes more trusting,
he can free himself to become more spontaneous, more inter-
dependent, and more freedom-giveing." (2).

"The core of the theory of group development is that
the principal obstacles to the development of valid communication are to be found in the orientation toward authority
and intimacy that members bring to the group." (3)

I'm not accusing the Sensitivity Trainers of being any-
where near as verbose and jargonistic as academics like,
say, Talcott Parsons (heaven forbid!). But, come on guys,
practice what you preach! Loosen up! Cut the B.S!

Trainers do have valid claims to make: In each case
where a participant has learned to like other people a bit
more. In each case where a person has come to feel better
about himself or herself and more comfortable with others.
In each case where a person has felt happy and has a
pleasant memory to look back on, has a good experience to
remember.

These are very, very valuable things to be able to give
other people. It takes professionals to manage the
situations which make them possible. And you deserve to be
paid for it.

So, yes. Let's have some more Sensitivity Training.
But, let's cut the c___ in the process.

REFERENCES

1. Argyris, Chris, "Explorations and Issues in Laboratory
    Education," National Training Laboratories, National
    Education Association, Washington, D.C,. 1966.

2. Gibb, Jack R., "Climate for Trust Formation," in Leland
    P. Bradford, Jack R. Gibb, and Kenneth D. Benne, <u>T-Group</u>
    <u>Theory and Laboratory Method</u>, John Wiley and Sons, Inc.,
    New York, 1964: 15-44.

3. Bennis, W.G. and H.A. Shepard, "A Theory of Group
    Development," Human Relations, 1956; No. 9: 415-437.

Kurt W. Back, James B. Duke Professor of Sociology at Duke University, has conducted research in group formation and social change; the measurement of interpersonal group and elite communications; the interrelations of psychology, demography and history; and the social psychology of culture. He is the author and coauthor of many books, including Beyond Words: The Story of Sensitivity Training and the Encounter Movement *(Russell Sage, 1972).*

7

"I have always depended on the kindness of strangers."

Kurt W. Back

The rise and decline of the encounter movement is the history of a technological innovation. Some followers of this movement may even call it the most important invention of the century. But one can also see that encounter groups are distillations of cultural trends which have led to the exaltation of the here-and-now, self-realization and emotional intensity. This transformation and the reaction to it are as much a part of the history of the movement as the procedures of group action themselves. Encounter groups are thus a cultural expression. Other, contemporary cultural expressions can help in pointing up some of the aspects of the movement. Here we shall use the parallel development in literature and encounter groups as a framework for the history of relations of man and community during the period starting in 1947.

Drama and Sensitivity Training: 1947

In 1947 two events of cultural significance occurred. One was the production of Tennessee Williams' play, "A Street car Named Desire," which started a postwar development in American drama. The other was the first session of the National Training Laboratory at Bethel, Maine which inagurated the successful rise of the movement of T-groups, sensitivity training and encounters.

"A Streetcar Named Desire," one of the first postwar theatrical successes expresses the theme of the social impact on an individual when society shifts. Is it the ancestral home? Sexual encounter? The remnants of the family? New roots in new people? Blanche DuBois is uprooted from the traditional scene of her upbringing and caught up in the world of physical and social mobility where the old genteel arts of conduct are not valid anymore. Finally, she cannot handle the personal and sexual relationships; she is

abandoned by her family and is taken over into the professional healing process. Her exit line, "Whoever you are, I have
always depended on the kindness of strangers," portends a
different kind of personal relations, based on here-and-now
instead of long tradition. The National Training Laboratory,
and the movement which sprang out of it, tries to teach
people how to act with strangers, how to live in a world of
high mobility and new events, how to deal successfully with
these by modifying or even rejecting the interaction patterns
of social convention. The same question may occur to the
participants, many of whom have changed their community at
least once. Here too, the final way of finding one's way is
the reliance on the stranger, on being used by and using
strangers to learn and to find self-realization. Again,
personal relations are based on the here-and-now.

At the start we see the similarity of the predicament
described by the playwright and the behavioral scientist.
Symptoms of stress in the society are present in several
types of activities, and this fact shows the symptoms to be
important. One of these activities is artistic expression,
the way creative members of society, such as artists, try
to express and overcome the stresses which exist in the
present situation. Another is the birth of new social
institutions to which people flock in order to heal their
own problems and the problems of the organizations and
groups to which they belong. Such phenomena as the sensitivity training movement and current literature explain the
problems of society and the society itself, and also
elucidate each other. In this spirit we will approach the
question of the place of the sensitivity training movement
within society.

The main issue to which these symptoms relate is the
relationship between the individual and the larger social
unit, the society. The original purpose of T-groups, at the
beginning of sensitivity training, was to make people better
by working in the group context. The relative importance
placed on work in groups as opposed to individual development has been a feature of the history of the movement as a
whole, as well as the cause of many tensions within it.
This ambivalent concern about the place of the individual in
society has also been a feature of American culture during
the period under consideration and represents an enduring
problem in the society.

Individuals, Small Groups and Society

The crucial factor which we shall discuss here is the
function of small groups, of voluntary organizations or

other similar links between the individual and society. From Tocqueville on, observers of American society have noted the importance of these groups in shaping the national character and contributing to the functioning of the society. The existence of these groups, their importance and personal enjoyment in addition to their value in furthering specific aims, has been a key to social development. Organization and management of these groups have become standardized. These skills are more wide-spread in this society than in most others. The rules are succinctly represented in Robert's Rules of Order, which are accepted implicitly as guidelines of all groups.

Faith in the control of society and in the ultimate benevolence of the community are integral parts of the American ethos. We have a basic optimism about the possibilities of concordance between individual needs and social requirements, a denial of the sense of tragedy has been shown in American drama even early in the century. A study by McGranahan and Wayne (1), an analysis of plays written in an earlier period, documented the strength of this faith. The study contrasted American and German plays written in the second and third decade of the century and showed that this feature was a distinguishing mark between the two cultures. The American play would always show the hero in conformity with culture. At most, a tragic or comic effect would result from a misunderstanding about the relationship, but the hero would finally see that society was correct and he would be readapted to society. In the German plays, the conflict between the two was unavoidable and the tragedy ended in the defeat of the hero by the forces of society.

A similar assessment made by Wolfenstein and Leites (2) in the study of movies mainly around 1945, compared American with English and French movies. The main thrust of American films is that winning is important and always possible. The conflict is always external; there is nothing in human nature and the hazards of life or society itself. This is in contrast to English films where human impulses are the principal danger, in an almost Shakespearan tradition, and the French films where the nature of life opposes human desires and the main human achievement is to accept losing gracefully. In the American films, life and society are ultimately benevolent and the dark side of human desires turns out mainly to be false appearances which are cleared up eventually. A kind of balance between the needs of the individual and society, is, therefore assumed in American culture and is essential for the functioning of society and the life of its members. Even when this balance is under strain, we might expect that some survival of this kind of of idea would be strong enough to be an important feature in any conflict of this kind.

We should not be surprised, therefore, that the technique of sensitivity training developed in this culture. Originally sensitivity training attempted to adjust a person to his group, having him work through the group to find satisfaction in adaptation to society. In a sense, sensitivity training, especially in its original formulation, is an expression of great optimism about alleviating this conflict. It is an attempt to show how application of simple techniques can help people to be trained to work efficiently within their groups, be happy within them and find both individual fulfillment and effectively integrated group life at the same time.

Small groups have mediated traditionally between individual and society in American life. If the whole fabric of relationships has become problematic, we should find that the value as well as the specific forms of the organization would be put in doubt at this time.

Man and Moloch

The original philosopher of the sensitivity training movement, Kenneth Benne, discussed the relationship of the individual and the group in contemporary literature. His work shows the connection between concern with the group, as treated in literature and the roots of the Sensitivity Training Movement. In his article "Man and Moloch," (3) he shows the conflict between man and the power of society as it is represented in four modern novels. The first of these, which treats the general problem in a somewhat abstract way is Kafka's The Castle. It comes from an earlier period and a European background, and is mainly introduced to show that the problem didn't spring up suddenly but gradually arose. The three other books, Malamud's A New Life, Heller's Catch 22 and Kesey's One Flew Over the Cuckoo's Nest, describe the individual's powerlessness and frustration in his relation to specific organizational situations, namely higher education, medicine and the military. Thew were written by American authors in the postwar period, and all three books achieved popular success. In each treatment the organization's goal is perverted from its original function: the college is merely interested in an efficient grading system and similar administrative functions, the army has become a giant business organization in which everything is for sale, and the hospital is mainly there for the expression of power of the hospital staff, especially the nurses. In each story, an individual tries

to make his peace with the organization by disregarding it
and finds that only through his own small group can he
achieve at least some amount of satisfaction. All three fail
but salvage some personal triumph in the general catastrophe
of their attempts. Levin, the hero of A New Life, drives
away with his mistress and her two children to some real life
of personal responsibility, Yossarian escapes to a mythical
Sweden which is a kind of imagined Garden of Eden, and
MacMurphy, Keesey's hero, escapes with death and transfigur-
ation. In all three novels, the organization, the combine,
the Moloch, as Benne calls it, is all powerful. The hero,
though trying for some adjustment, finds that the only real
solution is getting away completely from the grip of the
organization and its perverted purpose. There is still hope
of some solution, a small group, an purely interpersonal
relationship without any further goal but also without the
absolute freedom of lonliness. This is different from The
Castle, Kafka's novel, in which K. despairs that he can ever
come to grips with the organization and learn what it is for,
and nobody in the village is willing or able to help him.
There is no possible solution, nor attempt at solution, and
no escape. The Americans even at their most pessimistic,
still have hope that man can adjust to society and that the
present difficulties are just a misunderstanding. Kafka does
not see any hope of this kind. Benne, the author of this
analysis, is himself pulled between the optimism of the
society and the uneasiness of the time. A student of John
Dewey, that perfect incarnation of American belief in progress, he has also been active as a founder and close
observer of the beginning of sensitivity training. But he
also named his collection in which this essay appeared,
"Education for Tragedy." (4)

Drama and Doubts on Community

The postwar period, with the large army organization,
educational and welfare institution, in addition to big
business, met the confrontation between man and Moloch in
different ways. Here we can turn back to the stage, to
Tennesse Williams and "The Streetcar Named Desire."

Williams concentrates on a part of society where
reliance on group norms and group support has failed first,
namely the Southern plantation aristocracy. Blanche DuBois,
the heroine, has literally lived through the death of this
society, nursing the dead and dying of her family. She was
looking for release at first in contact with casual
strangers and in promiscuity, later in an attempted rescue
in the new society which her sister has been able to build
for herself. Finally, when even this fails and her sister

callously commits her as insane, she can still see her new
fate as a possibility of a new group. With her last line,
"Whoever you are, I have always depended on the kindness of
strangers," she follows the nurse and doctor to the hospital.
Perhaps, if it is a modern hospital, she might have a chance
for T-groups, role-playing and other techniques which can
make her forget the conflict between the individual and
society. Williams' second great play of this period comes
from the same background and proposes the same solution.
Amanda, the frustrated Southern belle in "The Glass Managerie"
sees the solution of her genteel poverty in telephone selling
or in getting a strange gentleman caller to her house. Both
are attempts at impersonal and somewhat ritualized group
action. When all fails, the son escapes into another company
of strangers as a member of a ship's crew.

Williams' characters lost something in the breakdown of
the safe, old group and tried to escape into another group
relationship however inadequate it might be. Another
popular, serious dramatist of the period, Arthur Miller,
deals in one of his plays with the difficulties underlying
this group orientation. Part of the tragedy in "Death of a
Salesman" is Willie Loman's complete dependence on interpersonal interaction. With unconscious irony he tries to
distinguish himself from his successful neighbor by saying
that Charlie is liked, but not well liked. Instead of being
well liked, Charlie and his son have some actual achievement
to their credit and do not depend purely on acceptance by
and interaction with others. However, being well liked is
not enough, as Willie's tragic end shows. The tragedy of a
man who only wanted to be well liked casts a fundamental
doubt on whether the kindness of strangers or even their
love is enough to take care of individual needs and
strivings.

Willie Loman's tragedy is an individual one. It also
represents a social problem. The salesman has died and given
way to the organization man. Sensitivity training and
encounter groups were attempts to help the organization man
survive, to give the individual a new security. We can
diagnose the reasons why this security was lost.

Social Conditions for Sensitivity Training

It would be a little too trite to blame the loss of
security in social relations on some global scapegoat such
as alienation. Some of the specific changes of society can
be identified; they are affluence, mobility, secularization
and belief in change (5). Rising affluence of a great part
of the population brought many persons to a point at which

they had thought that most of their troubles would be over.
It turned out, however, that neither this affluence nor the
satisfaction of at least some of their dreams brought
happiness. Further, the affluent society as a whole made it
possible to draw interest away from production problems in
general and toward niceties of relationships within society.
We are reminded here again of Willie Loman who could have
produced things and would have been happier then, but this
effort was not called for anymore. Affluence also enables
orgainization to give time and finances to help support the
sensitivity training movement.

The same part of the population which had become
affluent during this time, business men, white-collar
workers and professionals, were also subject to great
mobility. Many people did not live their whole lives in one
community, even had little sense of community, but were
moving from job to job and eventually were able to settle
in the "sun-belt," following favorable climate. The great
mobility trend of the middle of the century was in large
part a middle class mobility. People moved from the
Northern cities to the Southwest and West, and these of
course were the areas where sensitivity training flourished.

A third source of support which was being lost was
traditional religion with its function of giving meaning to
life and emotional release. With the growth of science,
religion lost its intellectual function of explaining the
world, and this introduced the possibility of a natural
experiment. Before now, the intellectual and emotional
parts of religion were never separated in a society, and
therefore we had no other possibility the emotional functions
were by themselves. If they are needed, and they seem to be,
the justification cannot come from religious beliefs or
mythology anymore, but must be based on science. Hence we
find new movements which look for the ritual and emotional
release of those mystic experiences, but try to keep a
bases in scientific respectability.

The fourth factor, perhaps the result of all three
previous ones, is a general societal belief in change,
regarding change in itself as the greatest good. Something
new and different or something which is changing is good
by itself and better than something old, the same or stable.

We can see how these four conditions disrupt community.
They counteract tradition by creating a mobile, secular,
intellectual class. However much the members of this group
have gained, they have lost or rejected this anchorage and
have "double-parked." Sensitivity training can be seen as

as a direct attack on this predicament. It takes the
dissatisfactions of the affluent society, insecurity about
life's stellar goals as well as unsatisfying personal
relationships. There are the conditions which have
undermined the belief in the balance between individual and
society and induced people to look for new ways of establishing this balance. T-groups, sensitivity training, and
encounter promise a new method of giving an instant solution
to these problems. The successes of the movement as well as
the tensions within it illustrate both the difficulty of
reaching a new balance and the trends which have occurred in
our society. Sensitivity training, therefore, starts where
the plays of the immediate postwar period left off. It
presents new ways for the mobile, secular person to accept
the community, to find "kindness in strangers," or to get
satisfaction out of "being well liked," or living without
being well liked.

The Story of Sensitivity Training

Sensitivity training at its inception in 1947 found a
tool which seemed supremely fitted to this condition. The
principal feature was a group whose content of activity
was its own process, which relaxed or abolished the usual
norms of interaction; which stressed "feedback" (the
immediate, detailed discussion of what happened) and which
used these techniques to produce a strong emotional impact
on its members. These techniques give the mobile, secular
person a sense of temporary community, they give the
affluent a chance to use his leisure in pseudo-productivity,
and they represent an ideal framework for change for its
own sake.

As a symptom of society, sensitivity training developed
with it. Benne, (6) who showed so well the basic conflict
between man and Moloch, has also described the early history
of the sensitivity training movement until its standardi-
zation in the T-group.

The T-groups had its own development in which the
question of whether the individual and organization could
keep a balance could not be avoided. After the first few
years at Bethel, there was a tug-of-war, one in the direction
of creating a pure group training center, the other a more
psychiatric-oriented one with a slogan of "Psychotherapy
for Normals." Both of these tendencies did not go to the
whole extreme; the idea behind the T-group, namely of
keeping the balance between the individual and the group
life, kept going. However, in the meantime, The National
Training Laboratory itself became so big that it has been

called, with some justification, the General Motors of
sensitivity training, a new Moloch made out of anti-Moloch.

We can continue the history of sensitivity training
beyond Benne's essay. After the heroic period which he
describes, the shape of group training settled somewhat into
a ritual. Not many innovations occurred for a few years. A
new upsurge of interest in this phenomenon occurred in the
early '60's as a counter-movement coming from the West coast,
in contrast to the East-coast centered Bethel movement. It
used the theory of encounters and was mainly directed toward
the individual, the liberation of the individual from group
pressures and even from the prison of his own body. This
branch of the movement has been fittingly called the human
potential movement, looking less for the group than for the
development of the individual.

The explosive development of sensitivity training during
the '60's would seem to be a symptom of some underlying
problem of society. Sensitivity training during this time
developed from a somewhat specialized group or individual
technique to a big industry. It includes on one side
consulting to business, government and large organizations in
introducing efficient systems of production and organization,
and on the other side a new industry of psych-resorts, of new
places for finding new styles of living, recreation and
direction. The problem of man and Moloch does not admit of
the easy solution of finding a little group for oneself or
finding a Utopia where individual and group life is
integrated. These attempts themselves become Moloch's giant
combine with problems of budget, organization and leadership.
In fact, adjustment to group life becomes a commodity being
traded by the combine as defense, education and health were
in the stories discussed earlier.

The Crisis of Sensitivity Training

The explosion of sensitivity training led to a crisis.
The different organizations sponsoring it struggled with a
number of issues. Should the group efforts remain middle
class oriented or should they be more directed to the
solving of social problems of deprived groups? Is the training possible in isolated weekends or single weeks or does it
ask for commitment to a total way of life? Can social
organizations stay within their old pattern to use sensitivity
training as a tool or must they be completely transformed?
Can the theory be based on a conventional framework of
science and research or must it reach for a non-conventional
means beyond science, beyond reason, and become involved with
irrationality and occultism? All these problems resolved to

the main one: To what community, if any, can the encounter
movement re-integrate its followers? The resolution for
these questions is foreshadowed in literature as was the rise
of the movement.

Literature of the Fifties and Sixties

Tony Tanner (7) in his analysis of American literature,
for the relevant period, between 1950 and 1970 has shown that
the principal conflict occurs between two poles: freedom and
structure. On the one side the authors see an unstructured
amoeba, the complete blob of no constraints at all, and on
the other side the total robot, the mechanical control of man.
The attraction toward and fascination with agents which are
ambiguous in this respect, which promise both enslavement
and complete release, such as drugs or occultism, is a case
in point. The writer of the '60's is fascinated with the
concept of entropy, the contrast between energy as organized
in individual points, and the even random diffusion of energy
leading to death and the end of the world. He tries to find
a way out of this dilemma by the use of language, by using,
as it were, style and communication as negative entropy and
in this way get control of the conflict. This conflict
represents the individual versus society tensions carried to
the logical extreme, and the writer tries to get control of
the human predicament through his craft. It is no wonder,
therefore, that so many of the heroes of current novels are
writers and that play with words and language attracts so
many of our novelists. Such writers go beyond Joyce whose
play with language had been so difficult for an earlier
generation. Nabokov makes elaborate variations of languages
within languages, and Walker Percy alternates between essays
on Peirce's theory of signs and novels which express these
theories. Further, many novels are monologues, therapy
situations in which an isolated person tries to think out
his own problems without any relationship to society at the
time. We need only to think of the situation of Portnoy's
Complaint, The Tenants, A Month of Sundays and Lancelot.

Therapy and writing are two metaphors by which the
novelist of today can discuss the predicament of the relation
ship between individual and group. This approach, however,
is intellectual; further, the strict therapy approach is
actually one which the encounter group movement has opposed.
The encounter group itself has not been used as a topic or
scene for modern literature. All fiction can do is to use
the encounter group almost literally as a scene where
different characters can be shown or as an element in a
satire of current preoccupations. At the peak of the movement, some theatrical performances used realistic group

therapy sessions and tried to involve the audience as
participants. Some examples in different media are The
Lemon Eaters by Sohl, a novelistic description of a marathon
group, "The Concept," a dramatic presentation of a synanon
group by casts of members of a drug treatment center and the
satirical film of an encounter group, "Ted and Carol, Bob
and Alice."

Literature of the Seventies

We can look again at the literary scene for a clue.
Perhaps the most significant development in the standard
American (Broadway) drama was its dominance by English
imports. This in itself may be significant, showing that the
American dramatist could not see his way out of the social
impasse and needed the impetus from a similar society.
Certainly the leading American playwrights of the earlier
period, Tennessee Williams and Arthur Miller, had subsided
by the late sixties, the main serious newcomers, William Inge
and Edward Albee concentrated on family relations, perhaps
an accompaniment to the nascent women's movement; other
dramatists were carried away by the immediate political
struggles. Thus the way for the discussion of community was
left to the English playwrights who introduced a new slant.

The dominant English dramatist starting in the sixties
on Broadway was Harold Pinter. We can charaterize his plays,
from our perspective, as descriptions of failed encounters.
Pinter's characters exist in a kind of limbo. Although they
have a past and constantly refer to it, they keep changing
it. Their interaction depends on their incomplete biograph-
ies which seem to be determined by the needs of the current
situation. The situation, is however, not a complete
encounter. There is always an ominous threat from the past
which leads to disaster. Overall the plays bring the doubt
that the here-and-now has any value, but in addition there
is also a doubt about any community in the past or future.
Pinter recognizes the search for community, but he can see
neither a safe reliance on one's background, nor an easy
solution in a temporary encounter. The title of a late play,
"No Man's Land" is a description of the setting of all his
plays.

The English playwrights did not feel strong loss of
community, but their attenuated struggle caught the current
mood. It is significant that the politically motivated
plays from England did not become an integral part of the
American stage. The plays which succeeded looked for a
bridge out of no-man's land. Examples of these attempts are
Tom Stoppard's verbal pyrotechnics, reminiscent of Nabokov,

and David Storey, who finds occupational groups and their
activities as fragile communities, in his plays on contract-
ors, rugby teams and art schools in contrast to the family
setting of his other plays. In two plays of the mid-seventies
the English mood seemed to have hit its American counterpart.
Shaffer's Equus goes back to the model of therapy which we
have seen earlier, but here the therapist is on the couch.
The psychiatrist yearns for integration into a mythological
Greece, but he can only cure his patient who has achieved a
life in the myth, into acceptance of the current atomized
world. The other, Simon Gray's Otherwise Engaged shows the
hero trying to avoid all community, with family, friends,
lovers. All he wants to do, and what he finally succeeds
in doing, is to listen to a recording of Parzifal, in a
vicarious quest for the brotherhood of the holy grail. The
drama of the seventies escapes the dilemma of the encounter
in two directions, by the acceptance of a long range, even
traditional group, or by retreating into the personal self.

Conclusion

The approach to community on the American stage in the
years since 1947 can be used for interpretation in the
meaning of sensitivity training. The attempts to obliterate
the line between the audience and the actors reached their
high point in the late '60's and was succeeded in the next
decade by the traditional play, similar to the decline of
sensitivity training and encounter. These were transformed
from an end in themselves to traditional therapy and training
techniques or faded out completely. Community was to be
reached in different ways.

The decline of the movement becomes an important cultural
symptom, just as its rise had been. After the arrest in the
transitional stage of community, integration, the liminal
stage of Turner (8) and Fernandez (9), the cultural pattern
tended toward the two alternatives, integration into a
temporally and spatially extended community or contracted to
the individual. The latter course is shown in the narcisism
implied in the fascination with one's body, diet, looks, and
condition on which many current observers have commented
(c.f., Fairlie, 10). The great popular outcries of 1977
have been against the banning of saccharin, which may force
people away from a self-imposed diet.

The other alternative has become an even stronger
cultural trend. The resounding success of Haley's Roots

television play, novel or history - has exposed the need for
belonging to a larger community, extending over generations
and into several continents. Roots, of course, was concerned
with that group in American society who had been forcibly
deprived of their community. It is reasonable that here we
find this strong rationale of generational continuity.
However, the search for roots has spread to all kinds of
ethnic communities and a number of guides have been
published to show how to design a family tree. Perhaps as a
climax to this trend, it has been announced that Debrett's
Peerage has established an office in New York, an ironical
sequel to the Bicentenial.

Sensitivity training started with the discovery that
intense emotional interaction with strangers was possible.
It was looked at, in its early days, as a mechanism to help
reintegrate the individual man into the whole society through
group development. It was caught up in the basic conflict
of America at mid-century, the question of extreme freedom,
release of human potential or rigid organization in the
techniques developed for large combines. Literature has
pointed the way to the coming development: we can find new
strength in tradition or concentrate on the private need of
the person. New problems in the society will produce new
ways of looking for a balance between the individual and
society. We shall not go to the logical extremes, but try
new forms.

REFERENCES

(1)   McGranaham, D.V. and I. Wayne, "German and American Traits Reflected in Popular Drama," Human Relations, I, 429-453.

(2)   Wolfenstein, M. and N. Leites, Movies, A Psychological Study, Glencoe, Ill., 1950, The Free Press.

(3)   Benne, K., "Man and Moloch" in Education for Tragedy, Lexington, Ky., 1967, University of Kentucky Press.

(4)   op. cit.

(5)   The description of the conditions and growth of the encounter movement to 1972 is described in more detail in Back, K.W., Beyond Words, Russell Sage, 1972 and Penguin, 1973.

(6)   Benne, K., "History of the T-group in the laboratory Setting," in L. Bradford, I. Gibb, and K. Benne, T-Group Theory and Laboratory Method, New York, 1964, Wiley.

(7)   Tanner, T., City of Words, New York, 1971, Harper and Row.

(8)   Turner, V., The Ritual Process, Chicago, 1969, Aldine.

(9)   Fernandez, J.,"Passage to Community: Encounter in Evolutionary Perspective," in In Search for Community,

(10)   Fairlie, H., "The Lost Art of Enjoyment," The Washington Post, April, 17, 1977.

Index

173

HM
134
.I5
1978

In search for community